Consulting for
Organizational Change

Consulting for
Organizational Change

by Fritz Steele

University of Massachusetts Press Amherst 1975

Contents

I should like to thank my friends, colleagues, and clients for their help and teaching. Some who helped in the specific preparation of these essays are Richard Walton, John Thomas, Barry Oshry, Robert Luke, and Deborah Jones.

1. The Consulting Function

There was a time when organizations and groups saw the use of an outside consultant's help as a last resort. If it were vital to getting a task done, then they would hire a consultant; but they would do so grudgingly, feeling that they were admitting to the world at large their inadequacy because of their inability to handle that which they would "normally" be expected to do for themselves.

Happily for me and others whose profession involves some sort of consulting function, this view of the consulting process shows some signs of becoming a thing of the past. The process of receiving professional help in various aspects of the organization's functioning has become a common event, one not really tinged with any particular suggestion of abnormality. This is not to say that people do not yet have mixed feelings about asking for or accepting outside help (I suspect these kinds of feelings will exist for as long as there is more than one person in the world); only that using a consultant is considered more a part of the normal process of work.

In some instances, the pendulum has swung in the oppo-site direction, and there is sometimes a stigma of defen-siveness or overextension applied to systems which consistently try to function entirely through the aid of inter-nal resources, with no recourse to the less involved and more specialized views that an outsider can bring to a problem situation. I personally do not believe that a group or organi-zation will make particularly good use of consultants if it feels that it *must* have them for display purposes, any more than it would make good use of consultants if it felt that they must not be hired at all. There must be a realistic choice based on some need that cannot be effectively or efficiently filled by someone immediately involved in the task of the moment. When this need is recognized, it can be met by a consulting process which is now a much more familiar and regular part of many organizations' lives than it was ten or fifteen years ago.

Naturally enough, this familiarity brings with it a great increase in the number of people who are playing some sort of role as a professional consultant or helper. The number and size of management consulting firms have steadily increased; specialized technical firms, such as information science or light technology firms, are in full swing and finding good markets for their services among firms who cannot develop capabilities in those specialties on the inside; and more people within organizations are being asked to serve as observers, critics or specialists to other groups within the system itself.

As is usually the case in a new area, analysis and development of systematic observations of the factors that influence the consulting process tend to lag behind the sheer increase in consulting activity. This collection of essays is an attempt to close the gap a bit by examining some aspects of the consulting process that I feel have been overlooked to date. In writing this book I had an eye toward both influencing the effectiveness of persons in consulting roles and stimulating further analysis and research on the dynamics of planned change and the helping process. More will be said about the nature of the chapters in a moment, but first I shall start back at the beginning, with a definition of consulting.

Consulting as a Function

When I refer to consulting, consultant, or consultation in this book, I intend the emphasis to be on a particular process, not on a strict occupational role. By the consulting process, I mean any form of *providing help* on the content, process, or structure of a task or series of tasks, where the consultant *is not actually responsible for doing the task itself* but is helping those who are.[1] The two critical aspects are that help is being given, and that the helper is not directly responsible within the system (a group, organization, or family) for what is produced.

This is a very broad definition which includes many activities. A behavioral scientist trying to help a group improve its interpersonal process fits both qualifications. So does an observer from department A as he shares observations with department B on B's six-month plan. So, too, does a structural engineer called in to assist the engineering department of a company in their work on a particular assignment. But a structural engineer who is subcontracted to *do* the project is *not* a consultant, since by my definition he (or his team) has become temporarily a part of the line organization of the system which hired him. For the same reason, two partners on a project may provide each other with help, but they are not consultants to one another, because the help is a part of doing the task for which they are both responsible.

Using this definition, consulting is a *function*, not an occupational role per se. I have tried to write this book in a manner that will be helpful not only to professional consultants, but to the many other persons who serve in consulting capacities at various times.

In practice, of course, the way I think about consulting and the examples I use here are not so open as the last statement may imply. The essays tend to be biased toward two particular aspects of the consulting function:

1. I tend to emphasize consultation that is aimed at *some improvement in the future functioning of the client system,* rather than simply at getting the immediate task completed satisfactorily. I emphasize this because

1. I use *task* here in a very global sense to include anything a person, group, or organization is trying to do. This covers a range including a corporation developing a market plan, a family trying to improve the way in which they deal with one another at the breakfast table, and a single person experimenting with how he can enjoy music more. Any of these tasks could be helped by consultation.

I believe that the total impact of the consultant's contribution is greater if it is cumulative, due to improved process or structure, than if it is specific to only one task at one time.

2. I tend to use *behavioral science consultation* as a model for many of the examples in the book. This is partly because my own experience is in this area, and partly because I see the applied behavioral science consulting process as the one that has most emphasized the improvement of future capabilities of the client as well as accomplishment of the immediate task. This does not mean that the discussions are not relevant to other types of consultants or to persons who are temporarily performing this function for someone else. On the contrary, I believe that many "expert" or technical consultants fall short of their potential contribution to a client because of their lack of attention or understanding of the process of change itself. The best advice in the world will not be used by a client if he rejects it for defensive reasons, or if the client system is not organized properly for using the help. Thus I feel that technical consultants would profit from this book and other experiences which make them more aware of their own choices of process and the way these choices directly influence the nature of interaction between themselves and the client.

Consultants' Roles

When a person is functioning as a consultant, what kinds of things is he likely to be doing? One way of briefly describing these activities is to think metaphorically about the various roles a consultant might play in a client system, that is, traditional roles which would be descriptive of his behavior within or his function for the client system. The following are role metaphors that have helped me see more clearly what it was that I was actually providing when I was functioning as a consultant.

Teacher. At times, my main function has been simply to

teach behavioral science theories or practical applications to clients. I use didactic processes, such as seminars, and experiential processes, such as short laboratory training sessions; but in either case I am defined as the teacher, and clients are the students.

Student. As well as being the teacher, there are situations where my most effective role is as a learner or student. As I will discuss in the chapter on learning from consulting, this is a useful role, because it both aids future consultation and models a learning role that I hope to transfer to the client: I hope to make him more curious about human behavior and more of a student of how things happen in groups and organizations. My best vehicle for demonstrating that is to be visibly engaged in that role myself.

Detective. I am often engaged in a kind of detection process, trying to discover evidence and fit it together in ways that will help me and the clients develop accurate pictures of the system, its problems, and its strengths. Because of its emotional potency, I chose this role to describe in detail in the chapter "Consultants and Detectives."

Barbarian. One of the reasons why human systems are not always self-correcting (i.e., able to readjust when they slide into ways of working that are not optimal) is that stable norms develop about what a "good" or "civilized" person ought to be like if he is to be a member of the system. Some of these norms facilitate productivity, growth, and enjoyment in the system; and others merely provide predictability or security, often at the cost of productivity or growth. As a consultant, one of my most important roles is to be a violator of comfortable but limiting norms: to be a barbarian who does not behave so politely as the rest of the members in the system. For instance, most groups develop taboos about openly discussing such issues as salaries or inadequate performance. As a barbarian, I often raise these issues, particularly if they are central to the group's problems. Not only does it help the group to deal with the issue (which is otherwise out of bounds and incapable of being influenced), but it provides a reflection to the group of their own self-created boundaries. I try to facilitate a process where they reexamine those boundaries and push back the ones that are blocking them excessively. Technical consultants serve as barbarians by questioning accepted ways of thinking about a problem area and not accepting the conventional wisdom which everyone inside the system thinks of as proper and right.

Clock. There have been projects where my most important role seemed to be that of a timer or clock for the client system to watch. When there was a regular schedule of visits that I would make to a system, I felt a bit like one of the little figures that come out of Bavarian clocks as the hour is struck. My presence (or the thought of it coming soon) served as a spur to clients to be thinking and experimenting so that they would have something to show me for the time in between my visits.

Monitor. Related to my role of clock is the role of monitor, where my function basically is to observe the client in action and to provide an independent view of how I see him operating according to standards which we mutually agree are relevant to his problems and aspirations. I serve as a monitoring system set up and calibrated according to some model of effective task behavior.

Talisman. Another function of my presence in a system actually has little to do with what information I provide in my observations. In my role as talisman it is the *fact* of my presence that is important. This fact provides a sense of security and legitimacy which allows the client to feel comfortable enough to experiment in areas where he might not act without support.

Advocate. Another role I often play is that of an advocate of the values or principles of relations between the organization and the individual. There are certain fundamental qualities which I feel this relationship must have in order to be decent, nonexploitive, personally satisfying, and productive for both; and as an outsider I am often in a better position than members of the system to advocate these values openly. Of course, if I become too consistently at odds with those principles valued by the clients, I shall lose my access to the system (by withdrawing myself or by being fired).

Ritual Pig. Finally, there have been instances where, in

retrospect, my function with a client system was to be a ritual pig.[2] By this I mean that I served as an outside threat which needed to be killed off (fired, challenged, resisted) in order for the system to develop enough sense of solidarity and potency to be able to begin some difficult self-change. I used to think that when my help was rejected, and a project ended in the early stages, that this meant no change would occur in the client system. Sometimes this is the case, but I have also seen instances where this event was the spur which drove the clients to begin to examine themselves in earnest. Hence my feeling of having been the ritual pig.

Stresses in the Consulting Function

There are, of course, many other kinds of roles which could be cited as examples of what a consultant is providing at different times. The ones that I have cited are those which have been most salient in my own experience. The acting out of these roles and others has developed in me a sense of the demanding nature of the consulting function, a feeling that there are some fairly specific stresses which go along with the consulting process. One is the *difficulty of measuring your degree of success*. Since you are not responsible for the task itself, how do you, as a consultant, measure whether or not you have made a difference, and if so how much of one? What criteria do you use? Some possibilities follow.

1. *The task was done well.* Could the client have done it well anyway? What was your contribution to it?
2. *The task was done quickly.* Did your efforts speed it or slow it? What will the speed of future tasks be like?
3. *Mr. X, the client, is grateful and says that you helped him a lot.* This is fine, but might this feeling also stem from relief at having finished with the consulta-

---

2. I say in retrospect, because it is very difficult to recognize this role while in the middle of playing it out. It is hard for me to discriminate at the time whether we are going through a sacrificial ritual, or whether my rejection will be the end of the process with the client really preferring the status quo.

tion, at having gotten out from under the scrutinizing eye of a teacher, a barbarian, or a clock?

4. *Mr. X and his group used a different (and better) process on the current task than they were using when you started with them.* Will they use it in the future, or was this for your benefit as a monitoring audience?

5. *You feel good about how you worked with the client and what you provided.* Fine, although it is possible that it was good for you but not for the client system.

The point is that the nature of the task of consultation means that feedback is often slow to come, and it comes in terms that may be quite ambiguous and difficult to measure accurately. In practice, measurement of effectiveness must be based on multiple criteria, including the quality and speed of accomplishment of specific tasks, the nature of longer term process trends in the client system, and the feelings of both clients and consultant about the change process itself. Data should also be obtained from a third party of some sort who does not have the vested interests of either consultant or client in making the consultation look effective or ineffective.

Besides the ambiguity of criteria of effectiveness, another major feature of consultation is the *variety and unpredictability of emotionally stressful situations*. When a person is functioning as a consultant, he is on the spot personally and puts his clients on the spot as well. When he is the teacher, detective, monitor, or barbarian, he is more likely to stir up anxieties, defenses, and resentments which will boil to the surface than if he comes into a system as, for instance, a supplier's salesman. The rules of consulting are not very well developed, and the areas he confronts are precisely those where people generally have some strong feelings; otherwise they would have dealt with them already. This means that the consultant must be ready to cope with emotionality in both the clients and in himself. Probably the most difficult demand is that he use this emotionality as data about the change process, even when he is in the middle of events and experiencing very strong emotional reactions himself.

The Style of This Book

In sum, the ambiguity and the emotionality make consulting a very demanding function, and they put special pressures on both consultant and client which make it difficult to learn from the process. This difficulty is really what motivated me to write this book. In it, I have tried to look at the learning process itself, and how it can be enhanced during consultation, as well as examine a number of other generally neglected aspects of the process. I am not presenting an integrated, single theory of the consulting function here, but rather trying to fill in large gaps which I think must be bridged before an effective theory can be developed. I have used a common theme, that of learning, in many of the chapters; but I see this as appropriate because it is really the business of life, not only of consultation.

In terms of methodology, the chapters that follow have very little of the literature review quality to them. Not much has been written on many of the topics, while others have more of a history. But even with these latter areas, I have not emphasized others' work, since my purpose was to explore new facets of these areas. The essays are based mainly on my own and my colleagues' experiences in consulting, along with observations, tape recordings of change activities and consultant team meetings, and some responses in the form of answers to a questionnaire from both clients and consultants. I used these various methods to do pilot research on the different topics, but this research usually shows up in the essays in the form of the ideas which it generated, not in quantitative tables or reports of findings. My own preference is to use research processes as a stimulus for new perspectives and for the rethinking of issues, rather than as studies which prove that X or Y or Z occur and how often.

By this description of my own style, I do not mean that it is not useful for others to focus their attention on research projects of larger scale which are more complete in themselves. There is a very valuable function which systematic researchers provide. I suppose that the test of whether my own preferred style is also valuable is the extent to which the rest of this book stimulates the reader toward new approaches, aspirations, and understanding of the process of consultation. I hope that it will.

2. Learning from Consulting

In this chapter I shall discuss specifically the processes through which consultants learn from their professional (and other) experiences. The consultant's role is one which is quite rich in the number and variety of experiences one can have while playing it. New situations arise almost daily, along with new possibilities for expanding one's skills. But it is not necessarily true that one *learns* simply because he *has* experiences. We know from work with client systems that it is possible, for instance, for a group to experience a certain kind of dilemma, to somehow temporarily reduce that dilemma to a tolerable size, and then recreate the same forces that led to the dilemma the first time. They had learned nothing about the causes of the problem and how to eliminate those causes. In the same manner, the pressures of the consulting role are such that a consultant may perform adequately in situations involving specific work and yet not derive much personal learning from these situations over a long term. I see special attention to a consultant's learning as of fundamental importance to him because of three observations:

1. There are special learning problems associated with the consultant's role, such as expectations from the client that the consultant have the answers and not be experimental himself; the consultant's self-image of competence, combined with the possibility of slow and often ambiguous feedback about success or failure which heightens anxieties about competence; and others which will be mentioned shortly.

2. In its essence, the consulting business today, for those consultants who are more oriented toward process, is concerned in the long run with helping clients and clients' systems become better able to *learn from their experience,* to use information from their own process to learn how better to influence or adapt to internal and external forces. Since the consultant will not be around for the vast majority of the client's experiences, his greatest leverage for long-term development is in the area of affecting how the client uses experience for his own growth.
3. Consultants, by and large, tend to be better at applying this conception of change to their clients' systems than they are at applying it to themselves. Like most professionals, it is easier for them to externalize a diagnosis and change strategy and use it on others than it is to admit it in themselves, no matter what their background or training.

It seems an obvious conclusion, then, that we need to do work in this area, to focus specifically on the aids and blocks to learning while performing the consulting role. I also have several personal reasons for this conviction. For one, I think that we *should* do better, as a way of living out in practice those values which we try to get others to test and accept. If we are not providing a model of an attitude of learning toward our own world, our exhortations and interventions are contradicted by the covert message of how we choose to behave ourselves. I also believe that only if we use for ourselves the techniques and processes we ask others to use will we remain in touch with the concrete *realities* of what it feels like to have someone observe us in a tense moment and reflect our behavior back to us in a "helpful" manner. If we do not, we should not be very free at proposing this as a strategy for others' own good. Finally, I believe that being a consultant carries with it unusual possibilities for excitement and learning which are greater than those found in most occupations. Learning and personal growth have been legitimized as a part of the role, and since this seldom happens, it would seem a shame to throw away that kind of opportunity.

This rather elaborate exhortation is simply a way of saying that I feel that learning is an important part of the consultant role, and that it is not necessarily easy. By learning I mean developing new skills, new views of cause-and-effect relationships, and new attitudes toward people, events and oneself. The rest of this chapter will consider, in three parts, the process of consultant learning: existenial dilemmas or polarities which can block learning, means of diagnosing one's own learning style, and personal steps which can be taken to enhance learning from experience.

Throughout this chapter I am using the term experience in a very broad sense to mean any situation the consultant participates in or observes which could alter in some way his own view of the world and himself in it. The situation may be related to work, such as observing and counseling a work group or collecting data on and diagnosing a whole organization. It also may be not directly related to work roles, such as, for example, an experience with family or friends. The point is simply that the process of life in general contains the potential for our learning from it or not, and that in the consulting role both the potential and the likely difficulties of learning increase. This should become clearer as I discuss some of the conflicting pressures in the consulting role.

Existential Dilemmas

Existential dilemma may be too grandiose a term to have much real meaning, but it is intended to communicate the feeling of being under conflicting forces which both help and block learning at the same time. I have selected several polarities which I think describe the special forces acting on a consultant as he performs various aspects of his role.

Performance and Learning

In its simplest statement, the dilemma of performance and learning means that if you always strive to perform tasks to the highest level of performance of which you are capable, you will tend to choose to do those things which you can do well already. Over a period of time this will result in relatively little learning of *new* skills, since those areas in which you could learn have been avoided in favor of those areas where you are already capable. This dilemma often seems to be experienced in the moment where the choice is between looking smooth and competent (by doing something well) or looking clumsy and incompetent (by trying something with which you do not have facility, and indeed cannot predict the outcome very well). I have sometimes described this dilemma as whether to show your *smooth face* or your *fuzzy face* to yourself and others.

When acting in the consultant's role, there are many pressures in the immediate situation (and in yourself) toward choosing the performance end (smooth face) of the scale rather than the learning end (fuzzy face). Clients expect you to be as competent as possible. If there are other colleagues involved with you on a project, anxiety about success of the project tends to make them expect that you and other team members will work on those aspects of the process which you can do best, not those where you need to learn. Consulting firms often experience this conflict in assigning younger consultants to clients; it is difficult for a man to develop if his specialty is all that he is allowed to do.

It is not only clients and colleagues who have expectations about performance. The consultant himself also wishes to feel competent and tends to avoid those areas where he will not immediately perform reasonably well. I think this is partly due to experience in the role of teaching and helping others. Practice as the "expert" makes it difficult to accept the reverse position of being the learner, where one tends to feel one down. Avoiding clumsiness is also a result of growing up in Western society where we are taught that children are people who need to learn, and that one can tell an adult from a child because he has learned something, and is now doing it. It is this view, for instance, that keeps many people from learning to ski or to ride a bicycle in later life if they did not learn these skills when they were young.

The dilemma in this situation is obvious, I hope: the more a consultant responds to his feeling in the immediate moment about wanting to make a competent performance, the more likely he will feel dissatisfied in the long run because of his lack of growth and development. He will reduce anxiety in each short-term instance, but simultaneously his anxiety about the long-term pattern will increase. In the extreme, a consultant who aims for only highest performance becomes a technician who applies the same skills to every problem. He may do it very well, but he is also susceptible to becoming obsolete and having the profession develop beyond his particular technical skill.

By the same token, the consultant who always opted for doing what he did *not* know how to do would not only be violating contracts with clients, he probably would not be learning very much either, since he would never be testing and reevaluating his knowledge. The proper balance is a mixture of the two, with the proportions depending upon the person and the situation, including the internal security of the consultant, the cost of a "failure" to the consultant and the client system, the availability of less risky ways of learning the same thing, and so on.

In terms of career patterns, this discussion would imply that consultant's feelings tend to push them toward an inadequate balance loaded too far toward the high-performance end of the scale.[1] Therefore I am suggesting that the consultant who wants to maximize his long-term use of his potential must be conscious of the process by which he chooses work situations. He must mix projects with potentials for high learning with high-performance projects if he is to grow. This is easier to write about than to do, yet I know that it can be done. The best evidence is my own observation of several senior consultants whom I greatly admire, each of whom has

1. The reader probably is aware already of the fact that what I am calling a "scale" from performance to learning is not a unidimensional scale with unique poles. In my view, a consultant cannot be really effective in long-term performance if he is not also learning; just as organizations often find that they have not maximized overall performance by suboptimizing on individual variables.

at times put himself literally in an apprenticeship role in order to learn about a new area in which he felt inadequate. That choice speaks loudly about the sense of internal personal security which these persons possess.

Perception of Open and Closed Systems

The dilemma of perception of open and closed systems is connected with the performance-learning problem (as are most of the those which I will discuss), yet it is more specifically concerned with conceptual views of the world and resistance to changing them. The dilemma is this: on the one hand, in order to work effectively as a consultant in a live interaction situation, such as when meeting with a client group, the consultant needs to have some sort of theoretical framework or set of assumptions which help him organize what he sees. If he does not have some conception of likely problems and cause-and-effect relationships in group behavior, there will be too many data for him to make use of them. So much happens in any social situation, especially in a work group with a previous history, that an observer must be selective if he is to develop a picture of the group and some notion of what kinds of changes it might need (not to mention how he might work with the group effectively). On the other hand, the more rigidly a particular conceptual scheme is held, the less likely the consultant is to see new patterns of behavior which are more relevant and important to that particular group. If he takes whatever happens in the meeting and pushes it till it fits his particular conceptual framework, then he is unlikely to learn about new dynamic situations which are truly different than the ones he expects to find.

The problem, then, is this: if the consultant has no model or system at all for analyzing behavior, he is unlikely to be able to make much use of his immediate experience, nor is he likely to learn very much from it, since there will be no cumulative growth in understanding a particular area. Conversely, if he has a single, tightly organized, closed system for thinking about organizational behavior, he is also unlikely to learn very much, since he simply throws away or distorts those data which do not fit the system. The former situation is analogous, in perceptual terms, to *not being able to focus* enough on figure-ground relationships to see a pattern. The latter situation is akin to *staring* in an effort to make the pattern emerge (also unlikely to help the perception process very much). The process which is called for is one of real *seeing*; of having enough of a previous model so that perceptions can be organized, but being flexible enough to let new patterns emerge and come into focus. My prediction is that the more anxious a consultant may be about whether he will be able to see something in a group's process, the more likely he will be to stare (to try to guarantee in advance that he has something to report), and therefore the less likely he will be to see what is actually taking place or to learn from it.

There is another aspect of the open-closed dilemma which I would like to touch upon. That is the difference between *new learning* (in an area where you have little previous experience) and *relearning* (in an area where you already have a set of attitudes or skills). The former is likely to be easier than the latter, since the "unfreezing" step will not require as much time and energy. For example, during a trip I made to England, the country changed over to decimalized currency. It was easier for me to learn this system than it was for many English, partly because I had worked on a decimal basis before, but also because I didn't have a firm rooting in the old system which would have to have been unlearned before I could use the new one. Conversely, when learning to drive on the left-hand side of the road, I had a very difficult time, because I had so many incorrect reflexes from so many years' practice of driving on the right.

For the consultant, the point is that he should be aware of when he is learning new things in a new area and when he is learning new things in an old area. For the new-new case he can take a relatively open stance. For the new-old one this will by nature be more difficult, and he should be aware of resistances to change or new views which are part of the unfreezing process. They are necessary but must be got be-

yond if the closed system conceptual scheme is to be altered
and new learning is to take place.

Finally, the open-closed dilemma also gets acted out in
the extent to which a consultant in the field relies upon
descriptive observations versus subjective inferences made
from those observations. The more closed your conceptual
system is, the more likely you are to use your subjective
inferences as if they were the original observations (which
they are not). For instance, if I hear a member of a group tell
another that he has made a good point, I can record just
that; I can also think to myself, "He's trying to draw the
other person into some kind of coalition," and record that in
my working notes. The latter is not an observation based
on what is happening outside myself; it is an inference
triggered by outside events, but it is mainly the product of
my internal conceptual framework which determines how I
interpret behavior.

In order to function as an effective consultant, we need to
have *both* observations and inferences available. The inferences often provide guidelines for actions which generate
reactions in the client group, which in turn give us better
data about the group. The problem comes in *confusing* our
own inferences with observations. The more we do this,
the less likely we are to learn much about how the outside
world works, since we are always seeing it in terms of our
already formulated scheme for interpreting behavior. This is
particularly true for cumulative learning over a period of
time from a single event. For example, I finally realized that
when I took notes which consisted of my inferences about
what I was observing, I could not very well use the particular
event over and over again for learning; I was the captive of
my original inference. I had not recorded what actually
happened in purely descriptive terms, so I had available only
my first inference, which made me generally unable to try
out new interpretations of what had actually happened.

For my own learning this was a very poor use of my experiences. I was building a collection of examples of my own
interpretations rather than experiences which I was observing. Now I try to record as much as possible what is actually

happening. For instance, when a boss points a finger at a group member and tells him something, I record it as just that, and thus leave myself free to go back and reinterpret it in the light of subsequent changes in the group or in my own way of looking at group behavior. I try to use both observations and inferences, but I try also to see them clearly for what they are.

Action and Processing

The third dilemma emerges from the necessity, if true learning is to occur, both to have experiences (action) and to work with those experiences (processing) to make generalizations from them which can be incorporated in your own repertoire of skills and attitudes. In other words, having experiences is a necessary but not a sufficient condition for learning, as is attested to by the example of anyone who gets locked into an ineffective way of dealing with a recurring situation.

The action-processing dilemma for a consultant's learning is usually caused by the emotional seductiveness of the action side of the coin. When there are many opportunities to do things which put you in contact with other people (usually people who reward you for being active and doing things), then it is difficult to take time out and postpone a new experience in order to process those you have already had. It is very tempting to move on quickly from one client to the next, and so leave yourself with little time for getting feedback from the old client, discussing your process with colleagues, making notes which help you sort out what happened, listening to or watching tapes, communicating experience to others, and getting their reactions. All of these activities produce less immediate stimulation than does getting out and "doing" another consulting event; yet the less energy you put into the processing activities, the lower the probability that you will learn very much that is new from your doing. Again, anxiety is probably a factor here, too. The more doubts a consultant has about whether he is accomplishing something, the more likely he is to fill his time with active types of activities, which at least provide him with stimulation and a short-term sense of accomplishment.

The point here is not simply that you must process your experiences in order to use them well. It also makes a difference *when* that processing occurs. We know from learning theory that people learn best from feedback which is closely connected in time to the actions they took which caused that feedback. This is why annual appraisal sessions between boss and subordinate may be useful only as symbolic ritual; they are often useless as learning experiences for the subordinate (not to mention for the boss!). The feedback he is getting is so distant from the original events that there is no way to invest any emotional or even theoretical commitment into using the information for learning. At best, the subordinate learns a bit about how to conduct himself at the appraisal interview, which is his immediate situation.

In a similar manner, the consultant who schedules his days and weeks full of client contacts and then takes off a few days to reflect (or goes to a course of some kind) is unlikely to be making very good use of his rich consultation experiences. When he gets around to looking at what has occurred, so many events intervene between the present and a particular experience that he can only scratch the surface of the meaning of the forces on him at the time and his internal reactions to those forces.

I think of the tight scheduling of active event after active event as a kind of *cramming* of experiences together versus a *spacing* of active events with enough slack so that the events can be used instead of just experienced. It takes some very active planning to move in the spacing direction, since both internal forces (anxieties, excitement) and external forces (client demands, new opportunities) tend to push the consultant into the cramming pattern of work.[2]

2. This requires such active planning that indeed we often avoid it and let work shape itself by whatever contracts come in. The best example that I know of an act of will to break this chain was the consultant who declared time bankruptcy when he recognized how overcommitted he was. Then he worked collaboratively with clients to redistribute his schedule and allow himself more opportunities for his own learning.

Threshold and Overload of Stimulation

The fourth dilemma has to do with the *intensity* of stimulation a consultant receives and its impact on his pattern of learning. In its simplest form, this can be described as the necessity on the one hand to have a high enough level of stimulation, challenge, and newness in a situation to reach the consultant's personal *threshold* of sensitivity, so that the experience will be real for him. There needs to be some sense of newness, of puzzle or difficulty, if a person is to feel motivated to try to learn from the situation. On the other hand, if this stimulation is too strong, too demanding or threatening, then the consultant will be most concerned about *survival* and will not focus on experimentation and learning from the situation. This picture of useful stimulation needing to be both high enough and not too high has been called the *U-curve hypothesis*. Schroder, Driver, and Streufert (1967) present a very convincing body of experimental evidence for the importance of both threshold and overload limits in human information processing.

What are the concrete applications of this to a consultant's learning? For one, it suggests that a consultant will tend to learn most from experiences that are challenging to him and somewhat beyond his present facility, but not too far beyond. If the situation is exactly that which he has been dealing with for some time, his experience is not likely to be above his threshold, and his curiosity and desire to learn are not likely to be engaged. Similarly, if it is a totally strange situation with high risk and high costs of failure, the stimulation is likely to be so great that he will again fall back on old behaviors that he "knows" have worked in the past. He is unlikely to generate experimental behaviors whose effectiveness he can test. Anxiety will also keep him from perceiving the events very accurately and will therefore distort conclusions which he draws from them.

Another implication concerns feedback from professional colleagues and clients. The U-curve conception suggests that feedback should be challenging enough to stimulate the receiver and yet not so challenging that it simply arouses feelings of being threatened and causes the receiver to close himself off to hearing the information. This latter effect can be reduced if there are messages of general support and acceptance along with the specific message about a particular issue or pattern of behavior on the receiver's part. If the message is one of total support, of course, then the threshold will not be crossed, and new learning is unlikely.

Internal and External Standards of Growth

In the previous dilemma of threshold and overload stimulation, the issue of where the threshold and overload of stimulation are is an empirical question which can be answered only by reference to a specific consultant at a particular point in his development. People are different in their tolerance of and need for stimulation, and they change individually over time. This raises the more general dilemma of *what standard* to use when examining whether or not you are learning at an appropriate rate. On the one hand, the field of consulting has so far not been well specified in terms of the necessary skills, knowledge of content, and attitudes which should be held by a "good" consultant. This generates uncertainty; and, in turn, anxiety about this uncertainty pushes consultants toward a comparative approach to measuring learning, where they compare themselves with other consultants, fellow participants in a training program, or whomever else is appropriate. On the other hand, this very uncertainty also speaks well for the nature of the field, and for the fact that there are widely different skills and areas of knowledge which can be useful. In addition, people learn at different rates and with different ends in mind, and this makes it more necessary to construct an internal standard to determine whether you are growing in the direction and rate which are relevant to your own time and needs.[3]

3. Although I am discussing it here as specific to consultant learning, I feel that the issue of gearing learning expectations to the needs and directions of the learner is the fundamental problem of education; and that most formal systems in this country push the learner much too far toward external standards.

Let me provide here an instance from my own experience which helped me to see this issue much more clearly. These are some notes I made after the event.

> I was running on the practice track at the gym today, and I noticed something about myself (and the others there) which has a parallel in my work. I was influenced in my workout by the rate at which others ran. When someone came round who was moving faster than I, I had a tendency to speed up and run closer to his pace. When I overtook someone going slower, I tended to ease off just a bit (and he seemed to speed up to match me). The thing that struck me was how inappropriate that comparison process was. I was running three miles and doing it for general shape and wind. I hadn't the faintest notion of how far either the faster or slower people were going, nor what their specific aims were while working out. This made them totally irrelevant as a standard for my workout, yet I am so tuned-in to competition that I let their presence change my own training pattern.

The point is that I think this parallels nicely the conflict between internal and external standards for professional growth. The external standards inherent in the comparative process of matching yourself to other consultants are very useful for getting a check on what is possible and how well you have done on a particular dimension. But, as a measure of quality of growth, it is as useless as my comparing my thirty-lap pace with that of a person running ten laps. Growth and learning are by necessity individual processes based on the potential and present state of the learner; and to use (and choose) his experiences effectively, a consultant must *run his own race*. That is, he must choose challenges and make experiments based on where *he* wants to go as well as on his own present level of competence, not on that of those around him.

I might add that consultant training programs make creating a run-your-own-race climate difficult, since people bring with them a high level of anxiety about how they will compare with others. But the implications are broader than how you behave in an organized program. Running your own race also suggests that you will be influencing your learning process by the kinds of projects you take on, and that this should be a personal choice based on what you want to learn, not on the basis of the thing that is generally being done at the time. One test would be whether you can take on "unfashionable" clients because of what your learning needs are, or whether you tend to stick with more acceptable clients even though you are learning nothing new with them.

Personal Security: A Common Theme

I have tried to summarize the discussion which appears above with the diagram shown in figure 1. The diagram depicts two major ways in which a consultant's own choices affect the nature and amount of his learning: the *situations* in which he chooses to put himself (A), and the *stance* he takes toward the experiences that result from those situations (B). How he handles the dilemmas I have discussed influences both of these areas of choice. His choice of situations is influenced by the forces of performance-learning, action-processing, threshold-overload and internal-external standards of growth. In the same manner, the main influences on the stance which he takes toward an experience tend to be the forces of performance-learning, open-closed, internal-external standards of growth and threshold-overload of stimulation.

The stance taken in turn affects the outcomes of the experience, namely what is done, what is learned, and how the consultant feels about the experience and himself. These outcomes feed back to influence future choices about both situations and stance.

There is one important outcome which is the main influence on the choice of both situations and stance. This is the consultant's sense of competence and his self-esteem. When these are low, he tends to feel anxious about how he will look to himself and to others. As the above discussions often indicated, excessive anxiety pushes a person toward nonlearning alternatives: toward performance and away from learning,

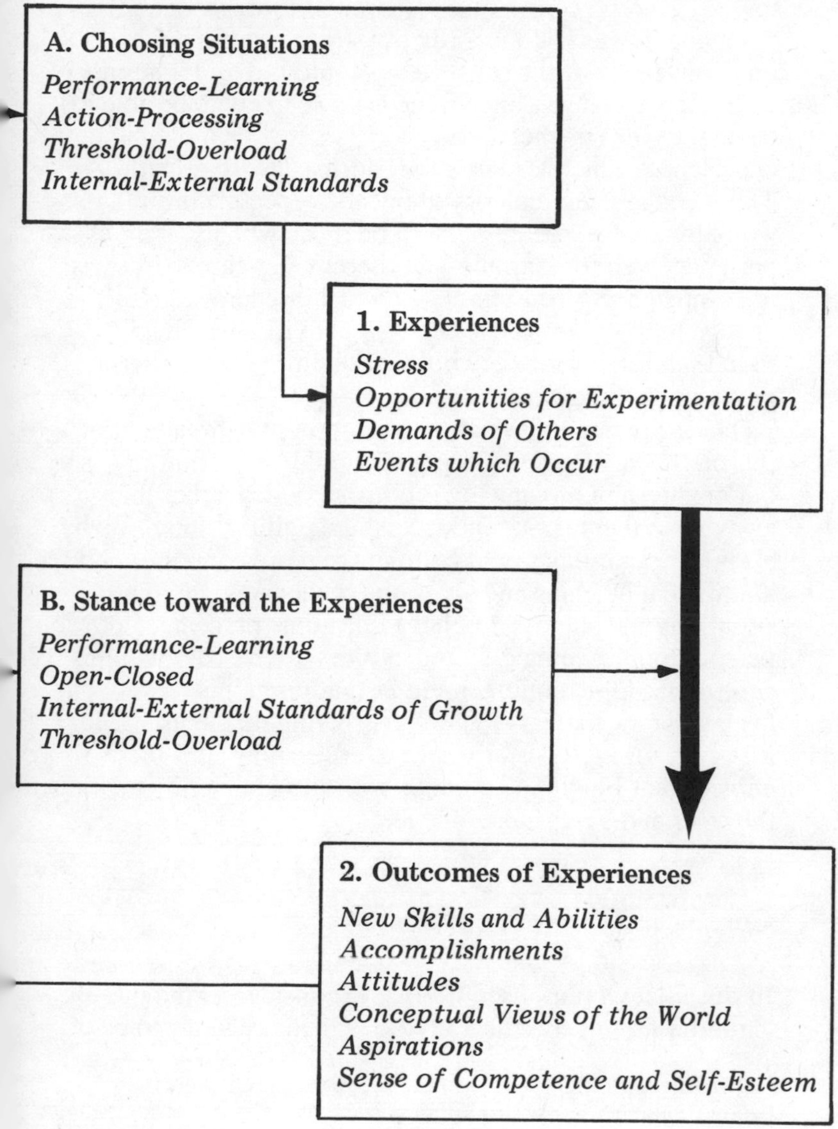

A. Choosing Situations

Performance-Learning
Action-Processing
Threshold-Overload
Internal-External Standards

1. Experiences

Stress
Opportunities for Experimentation
Demands of Others
Events which Occur

B. Stance toward the Experiences

Performance-Learning
Open-Closed
Internal-External Standards of Growth
Threshold-Overload

2. Outcomes of Experiences

New Skills and Abilities
Accomplishments
Attitudes
Conceptual Views of the World
Aspirations
Sense of Competence and Self-Esteem

FIG. I. Forces on Consultant's Learning

toward a closed conceptual system and away from a more open one, toward action and away from processing, and so on. Conversely, if the consultant should have a high sense of competence and self-esteem, he is more likely to be able to trade the gains of short-term successes for the more difficult experiences which lead to a long-term sense of growth. There is, then, a circularity about the process: consultants who already feel secure seem to be those who use their experiences well for learning and thereby increase their sense of competence.[4] Consultants who feel insecure seem to engage in more protective types of activities which will reduce short-term anxiety but will do little for long-term growth of competence.

There are ways in which a consultant may break out of this circle, however. One method would be for him to work out a pattern of moving toward his anxieties rather than away from them. A second is less like pulling himself up by his bootstraps: this would be to make more conscious choices about what he gains and gives up by choosing different situations and stances. I believe that some percentage of each person's nonlearning oriented choices are based not on his central need for reinforcement at that point, but mainly on his lack of awareness of what he is giving up by opting, for instance, for high performance over learning. It is these choices that I hope to influence with this chapter by making the costs and gains more visible.

Consultants' Learning Devices

In this final section, I should like to consider a kind of "laundry list" of specific activities which are likely to be of

4. Although I digress beyond the scope of this chapter, I also believe that there is a basic human need similar to White's competence motivation (1959), but one which is related to the sense of *change* (i.e., growth) in competence. I think that human beings by and large are aware of the rate of change of their competence as well as its absolute state, and that they find too low a rate of change to be dissatisfying.

use in enriching the learning that is obtained from consulting experiences. To many readers, the items may be all old hat; to others, some will be old and some new. The point in summarizing them here is that even when we "know" techniques, we usually think of them as devices which *the client* needs to use and fail to apply them to ourselves and our own development. Two main groupings will be outlined: activities related to self-diagnosis of personal learning style, and activities for increasing learning from consulting experience. Obviously these are not discrete categories, especially since performing the first effectively is a good means toward performing the second.

Self-Diagnosis of Learning Styles

Diagnostic questions. I have found that it is helpful to have a regular set of questions which can be used to help me decide whether or not I am using my experiences well. The following are the questions that have been most productive along this line.

1. Do I now have a conscious strategy for learning from my consulting activities? If so, what is it, and how effective is it? Where does it fall short?
2. What does learning mean to me? In what areas do I want to grow?
3. From what situations do I seem to learn? Which ones do I seem not able to use for learning?
4. What is my own learning style? Do I need to acquire large hunks of experience and then analyze them; small bits only which I then process; or do I learn best when I make some advance predictions and then acquire experiences which I check against the predictions?
5. What blocks learning for me? Is it a bad situation, or internal fears which keep me from using a situation well? Do I tend to avoid situations where I might learn something new or be forced to change my usual style?

6. What kinds of situations seem to give me pleasure and stimulate me? Which ones do I now find dull and unengaging?
7. From whom do I seem to be able to learn easily and well? From whom is it difficult for me to learn?
8. What ways do I use to get information about the effects of my actions in consulting situations? What new means might I use to get this kind of information?
9. In what areas do I care most about learning and changing? In what ways do I want to increase my competence?
10. How much am I really motivated to learn versus doing what I can already do well? When I look at what I choose to do, what does the pattern tell me about this?

Utilization of time. Another helpful analysis is one which we often suggest to overcommitted or inefficient clients: that they take more of a problem-solving attitude toward their use of time and energies. The same may be applied to ourselves. I have found it very useful to keep a running record for a period (usually at least two weeks to capture variations in schedule) of what I do, and particularly how I use my time. This can show up the cramming type of pattern very quickly and indicate ways in which one is systematically excluding activities based on learning from his day.

Life-planning exercises. Herb Shepard of the Yale University Medical School has developed a series of exercises which help one to look at his life with more perspective than usual. The exercises lead a person through an inventory of present activities and commitments and into an analysis of how he feels about these in relation to what he would *like* his future life to be like. When done systematically, these exercises exert a very emotional impact and can generate strong motivations toward change.[5]

5. The scope of this chapter will not permit me to reproduce the exercises here. The interested reader should contact Professor Shepard directly for a copy of them.

Recordings of one's own behavior. We have available to us today a wide range of technological aids to obtaining feedback on our own behavior. Especially helpful are audio and video tapes which can be used repeatedly, and which provide raw data rather than interpretations. These have been used a good deal in changing clients' attitudes, but the consultant can also make good use of them, particularly if he concentrates on replaying the incidents which were related to how he was using his experience for learning. If we do use tapes of ourselves, we usually focus on effectiveness of our influence rather than on learning behavior as a criterion; but tapes can show us very concrete instances of how our stance affected what we got out of a situation.

This also suggests another source of data: feedback from clients and colleagues. When we do get feedback from them, it is usually related to performance of some sort; but again there is no reason why, as observers, they could not be asked to look specifically at our learning postures as well. If some specific request along this line were made, it would not only result in data for yourself about learning style but probably would stimulate the observer to look at his own learning (and nonlearning) behavior as well.

Devices for Consultant's Learning

Finally, the following are some of the devices that I and other consultants have used to "stir the pot," that is, to enrich the experiences of consultation so that growth is experienced from them. As I suggested, many of them may be fairly obvious, but the issue is how much we actually use them on ourselves in contrast to using them on only our clients.

New experiences. One of the clearest implications which may be drawn from this chapter is that a consultant should look carefully at the experiences in which he typically finds himself involved, and he should widen his range of experiences to include those at which he is not greatly practiced. If most of his time is spent with small groups, it would be useful to find some larger-scale systems with which to work as a growth experience. If he always works with a particular kind of client, such as businessmen or government agencies, then some conscious planning should go into broadening that aspect of his experience. If he is always in a well-defined consultant's role that is clear both to him and to his clients, it would be instructive for him to try to be helpful in situations where he is not formally defined and accepted as a helper, such as in his own local neighborhood groups. The point is to diagnose the dimensions within which a consultant's experiences tend to be routinized and to find situations which provide more variety within those dimensions. In order to do this he will of course have to deal with those forces discussed earlier, which will push him toward doing that which he is used to doing.

Devices for feedback from clients. There is no substitute for a regular flow of feedback from clients to the consultant. This is not the only kind of information from which he can learn, but without it his generalizations will be unrelated to the actual effects of his actions with the client. This feedback will not generally happen unless the consultant encourages it and sets up devices to make sure it does happen. The device can be a temporal one, such as setting aside certain parts of a session for feedback, or holding special feedback meetings regularly. It can also be mechanical, such as providing the client with rating scales to fill out, a tape recorder on which to record his reactions, and so on. As I indicated above, what the consultant expresses interest in influences his results. So it is useful, if he wants to get data on his appearance as a learner, to ask specifically for this kind of data as well as for information about performance.

Collaborative consulting projects. There is also no substitute for the experience of working with colleagues who speak a similar language and are concerned about similar issues in the field of applied social science and planned change. I believe that I have learned more from discussions with fellow team members during a project than from any other single source. Yet the problem here has already been outlined: it is necessary that you and the other members care more about learning than about looking good at each others' expense. If that norm does not exist in a joint project, there will be strong pressures pushing toward performance at the expense of learning, for real learning means being willing to expose yourself and openly question areas in which you do not have advance knowledge. I have worked on some projects where we were in the comparison-performance mode and on others where we were in the internal standards-learning mode. In the former case, we each did those things which would gain praise from the others, and we performed well as individuals but not so well on the overall project. In the latter case, I and others felt more willing to experiment and accept help from others. I think that we learned more from the latter situation and actually performed just as well if not better for the clients, since we were modeling the stance that we were trying to get them to experiment with for themselves.

Research Projects. I will note here only that I have found research studies to be one of the best devices for a consultant's learning. I am convinced that when research is carried out, the person who does the study learns far more from the process than anyone who may use the results of the study. It is true that science is a cumulative process, but a lot of the accumulation comes about through the *process* of performing scientific work rather than simply piling knowledge on top of knowledge. The learning comes, I think, from having to be specific enough about what one is attempting to do and which are the significant variables in designing a study. The research process also generates a kind of curiosity which then feeds itself and again "stirs the pot." To this end it is not necessary to always do the research oneself. The same kind of excitement and curiosity (and data) can be generated by supporting others who would like to do research on the projects in which you are engaged. Consultants often resist being studied, seeing such scrutiny as an intrusion. I think that not only the researchers but the consultants themselves lose because of this attitude.

Professional development sessions. It is much easier to deal with a client's reluctance to take time out of a busy schedule to attend a training session than it is to deal with our own reluctance to attend self-development sessions. The pressures which are placed on us demanding performance, action, and functioning in the helper role rather than that of being helped, all make this choice difficult for a professional consultant. Yet it seems all too obvious that the consultant who is not periodically either attending an existing program or having one especially designed for him by someone else is probably avoiding the issue of his own learning process and how he is facilitating it. The difference here is between an attitude of taking whatever experiences come along and hoping that we learn from them and one of social invention which allows us to use learning resources wherever they might be and to invent those experiences that we need, but which have not happened by chance.

Short-time-cycle events. Along the line of social invention just taken, I want to mention as my last device the use of consulting situations that have a compressed time sequence; that is, where diagnosis, action, and feedback on results can be obtained within a very limited period of time. For example, in consultant training programs of the last six years, the NTL Institute for Applied Behavioral Science has been building in projects with real clients in the area where a program is taking place. These projects have a very limited span, possibly as short as a total of one week's running time. I will describe them in more detail in the chapter on the use of the laboratory method for training consultants. The point here is that short-time-cycle events should be sought periodically, because they maximize the likelihood of learning from the events. Action and its effects are connected in a manner which is much more difficult to see in a project stretching over two or three months or years. The consultant, if he is exercising control over his schedule, can gain from mixing in some short activities, because they provide immediate data to work on, and also because they help him practice *using* data for learning purposes.

Recognizing Patterns

In closing, I should like to add simply that this chapter was written in the hope that it would help readers to recognize their own styles of dealing wtih their experience and to improve those styles. The issue is not really what one does with any given event in his work life, but rather what does the *pattern* look like over longer periods? Are you choosing to systematically exclude certain kinds of situations from which you would be learning more than from your current projects? Are you systematically avoiding certain kinds of data or issues in the situations you do get into, so that you are not learning about those areas? For most of us the answer will generally be yes to these questions. The issue then becomes one of recognizing our biases and engaging in a conscious process of social invention to reduce them. It is this process which will expand our ability to use experiences for learning as well as for performance.

3. Learning and the Client's Role

The need to learn is obviously not simply a challenge which the consultant must meet in order to be an effective professional. Client learning is one of the fundamental goals for most consultations. The longer one works as a consultant, the easier it is to forget what the world of the client is really like. What does it feel like to pay someone to get you to change? What are the forces that help or hinder a client's learning as he tries to give attention to both the change project and the demands of business as usual?[1]

This chapter and the following one will briefly explore some of the more basic aspects of these questions. First there will be a discussion of the client's role and its implications for learning. The next chapter will deal with learning patterns at a social system level, where *organizational overlearning* leads to inappropriate learning applications. In addition, chapter five will deal in part with some training methods which enhance the client's ability to learn from his own process, and chapter eight ("Consultants and Detectives") examines ways in which consultants can be meeting their own needs and unwittingly blocking client learning.

Forces on the Client

To be a client is basically nothing more than to be in a position of receiving systematic help from someone defined as a

[1]. For the sake of convenience, throughout this chapter I shall refer to *the client* and *he* when discussing receivers of help. In practice, of course, there may be one or more clients, and they may be male or female.

consultant. In the process, however, there are certain features of this role of client which tend to block the very goal being sought, that is, they block learning new views of the world and new ways of behaving.

A *role* as defined by those involved in the social sciences is a set of expectations about the behavior and attitudes of someone who occupies a particular position in a social system. I will discuss built-in learning blocks by touching on three sets of expectations about what a client "should" be or do: (1) expectations which the client has of himself, (2) expectations which the consultant has of the client, and (3) expectations which other people in the client's system have of him.

Expectations the Client Has of Himself

Any client has a number of ideas about what he should be like in order to be acceptable to himself. The first and foremost probably stems from the basic need for self-esteem: he expects that by and large he will not be a fool. This expectation can stimulate goal-directed activities and greater efforts toward change and improvement.

Unfortunately, the desire not to look stupid or incompetent also has its negative side. This is the equivalent of the performance versus learning dilemma for consultants described in chapter two. The better a client expects himself to perform on whatever tasks he does, the fewer his opportunities to learn new skills. Part of the consultant's task is to provide support for experimentation and to make it legitimate for the client to be clumsy and unskillful.

Another expectation that clients usually have of themselves is that they will maintain or increase their influence and power. I have seen very few clients who felt that a decrease in their own power would be a step in the right direction. In general, there is nothing wrong with this stance, but in the extreme it, too, has its cost in lack of learning. When power becomes an end in itself, then success and failure are measured by the experience of increased or decreased power, not by the accomplishment of a task.

This in turn makes the client hesitant to accept activities

which produce change, because these will disturb the balance of power. The more unpredictable the impact on his power score, the more hesitant he will be to help the consultant rock the boat. It will also be difficult for the client to learn about alternative approaches to power distribution, since the experiment itself will seem like a loss in the power game.

In the United States and countries with similar cultures, clients are likely to share the norm of society that "weak" people need help and "strong" people can do their jobs themselves (the "Please, Mother, I can do it myself!" syndrome). When the client has internalized this cultural value, this obviously makes it uncomfortable to take the client's role; and a good bit of energy can be expended in demonstrating to the consultant that there actually is no real *need* for any help—it is only a convenience of the moment.

This attitude is a particularly significant block to learning when combined with our general cultural expectation that education and learning is for children and doing and knowing is what adults do. The consultant's task in this dimension is to expand the client's conception of learning as a lifelong process which is essential to growth and to encourage both giving and receiving help as signs of strength when they are done well.

Expectations the Consultant Has of the Client

In performing his role, the consultant sends many messages to the client which indicate what he should be in order to become an acceptable alter ego to the consultant. Each constellation of consultant role behavior implies a reciprocal role posture on the client's part. This matching process is necessary for the consultation to move forward, and yet there are also potential learning blocks built into the expectations for the client.

For illustrative purposes I will describe the reciprocal client role and the potential learning blocks associated with the three consultant roles of teacher, barbarian, and monitor.[2]

2. The impact of the detective's role on a client's learning is discussed in depth in chapter eight.

Teacher. When the consultant assumes the role of teacher, he implies that the client should become the *student:* he must be interested in learning, follow the lead of the consultant-teacher, and be responsible for having mastered certain areas of content. The trap here is clear: the more the client becomes dependent upon the consultant for definition of what the client must learn (rather than *how* to learn it), the less likely he is to develop internal standards of relevance which will help him to learn when the consultant is no longer present. The client may also deny his own wisdom about process as he defers to the consultant without much question.

Barbarian. When the consultant violates norms that have been generally accepted by the client system, the reciprocal client role might be called that of *sophisticate* or *good citizen*. The hope is that by being honest about his reactions to the consultant's deviance, the hidden controls and structures can be made visible and become legitimate topics for analysis and possible change.

The danger here would be the adoption of one of two stances: the client may take the sophisticate's role too seriously or not seriously enough. If he simply perceives the consultant as "not our kind of person" and privately writes him off as a resource, then there is no public revelation of hidden norms. The client simply finds a way to get out of the consultation, and the untested norms of the system remain sacred. If the consultant's behavior is too easily accepted as obviously all right because it is *his* behavior, then the present norms still remain hidden. When the consultant is present, he can get away with many things as a barbarian, but a lack of open confrontation leads to no new operating room for anyone inside the system.

Monitor. In the role of monitor, it is the consultant's presence which is the primary input to the client system. When he is present, he is a visible reminder of a set of values, processes, and goals for change. The reciprocal role is mainly that of *performer,* where the clients act and the consultant observes.

The consultant as monitor expects that the client will strive harder with the added incentive of being observed, and this often is the case. The negative aspect of this role comes from the performance versus learning dilemma. Not many people want to appear clumsy in front of a judge, especially if they admire the judge. The client may tend to do his best routines when in the spotlight, which covers up the very data that are most useful for diagnosing problems, and keeps the client from attempting those activities which he does not yet do well.

In addition, I have seen instances where a consultant's presence led to a group of clients raising issues faster than they could handle them. This is the reverse of the problem: instead of best behavior which does not reach a threshold of the client's problem interests, there are overeager performances which lead to overloads which the clients are not yet ready to handle.

There is clearly a tricky line here for the consultant to tread. His presence will be a stimulation for the client. If it is too little, there is less impetus for learning; if it is too much, the client will either cover up problems in his attempt to do well or uncover so many issues that a mood of disintegration or discouragement will be created. This balancing process is a particularly crucial area which needs free discussion between consultant and clients.

Expectations which Others Have of the Client

There are usually numerous other members of the client's work system to whom he must relate, and these will all have expectations of how he should behave in his role of client. Some of these will encourage his learning, such as when others show an interest in what is happening and its implications.

On the other hand, some expectations will obviously inhibit learning. When a person changes his behavior in an organization, those who related to him have to adjust to the change, and often the most tempting thing is to try to get him to return to "normal" or become his "old self." If a consultant intends to help a client learn newer, more effective behaviors, he must be concerned with a diagnosis of who now reinforces and encourages the less effective behavior. There is abundant evidence that learning which is not supported by adjustments in the person's environment is likely to be neutralized fairly quickly.

Sometimes the changes can be *too* well supported. The last few years have seen a massive popularization of psychology, particularly as it is used in encounter groups and other consciousness expansion processes. System members who are not involved in a consultation often send signals about their unrealistic expectations for visible, immediate change in the clients. These signals can seduce the clients into uncritical acceptance of new styles which do not really fit them and will have to be abandoned later. The consultant should help the client to accept (and be willing to disappoint) others' fantasies of how he should behave as an improved person.

Differences in Roles

At this point I should like to consider a basic difference between the fundamental natures of the consultant's role and the client's role. Their modes of taking the role are existentially quite different.

The consultant's role is usually placed in a professional occupation category. Those who play it think of themselves as *consultants* and refer to a body of expert knowledge, values, and standards of professional behavior. They talk to other consultants, attend professional gatherings such as the Organization Development Network meetings, and read journals and books which reinforce their own concepts of themselves as professionals. In work life, the role of consultant is often their most important identity.

The consultant's experience is very different from the experience for someone in a client's role. To begin with, the concept of *client* is an abstraction used by consultants so that they know how to refer to the people they are trying to help. Clients do not necessarily think of themselves as clients at all. They almost always have more important identities as businessmen, scientists, or government officials. Being a client may not only be not a first priority, it may be third or fourth or fifth.

Clients do not have a reference group of other prominent clients with whom they may identify. Clients do not usually have network meetings where they talk about the state of the art. There are relatively few materials which a client may read to help him learn about his role. His conceptions of how he must act are often the product of fiction or word of mouth, "war stories" he hears from people who have been through the experience, and his own fantasies about what a client would probably do in different situations. It is for these reasons that I recommend in a later chapter that laboratory training be used to help clients learn about their role; not because there is one best way to behave, but because the laboratory method can speed up an otherwise cumbersome and haphazard trial-and-error role development.

In a consultative relationship, therefore, a consultant may function in his primary occupational identity, relating to a client to whom the role of a client is a third- or fourth-priority identity. The client's level of awareness and concern for the consulting process would therefore be lower than the consultant's. This is clearly due to the structural differences in the roles, not to any particular perversity on the client's part. The client's apparent reluctance is often the result of a realistic ordering of priorities where the process of change fits lower on the ladder for him than do other major demands of the business.

Rather than trying to recognize the different stakes that the parties have in the game, the consultant often interprets slow action as simply resistance to change. Resistance is certainly a relevant concept and a possibility, as I will discuss in a moment, but this view attributes the feeling at issue to the *client* (who feels anxious about changing), when the root may well be in the consultant, who feels disappointed that the client does not share the consultant's zest for his top-priority activity.

Becoming a Client

It has often been very instructive to ask myself how one of my clients *became* a client: what was the history that led us to our present relationship, given the great range of possible things that each of us might be doing at a particular moment?

It takes effort to be in a client's role; no one gets that experience free of charge no matter what the monetary cost. This is effort that usually could be expended more easily in other ways, especially while dealing with the demands of business as usual. I have yet to discover a client who had the problem of not enough to do to keep himself occupied. So in order for someone to put forth the effort to become a client, there must be some strong counterforces against the push to deal with only the regular demands of the job.

The most obvious force is the client's feeling that something is wrong which won't go away. This is the classic "pinch" notion that is often used as the standard beginning of the seven-step (or five-step, or whatever) consulting process. If the client is in that role because he feels that it is worth a try, he usually is somewhat open to experimentation and other demands of the client's learning process as well as subject to whatever anxiety he feels about the future and the possibility of negative results.

With many clients, however, feeling a "pinch" is only one factor in how they became a client. For the majority of people who play client roles in organizations, I would estimate that a key force on them is that someone who is in a supervisory position over them desires that they seek consultative help. A key element (either conscious or unconscious) in the client's motivation in this situation is simply survival: playing the client's game well enough so that one does not attract attention to oneself.

This stance makes it difficult to learn from the consultation experience so far as improving the future functioning of the system is concerned. What the client learns quite well is the whole lore of playing the game: devising better and worse ways to show interest and still keep the consultative process moving slowly enough to be no real threat, keeping his nose clean, and making attentive noises which reduce the attempts to influence him of those above him in the hierarchy. Most of the learning is about the power of the boss and the consultant, and how it can be used to force other people into activities that are good for them.

All of this says only that in most consulting situations there is some element of coercion behind the client's choice to ask for help. The coercion comes from either the threat of a failing work procedure or from some people in power who think that the consultation should occur. In either case, the client himself is likely to have the mixed feelings that we have been discussing throughout this chapter. These mixed feelings do not mean that nothing can happen, but they do imply that the client may be more interested in surviving the client-consultant game than in what he can learn about his own operation.

There are two obvious ways to stop this game. First, something may happen in the consultation which really does help the client. For example, an intergroup confrontation could visibly result in fewer barriers between the two groups, which could lead a captive client to reassess his assumptions about what can be accomplished. Second, a consultant may also directly confront the question of voluntarism and the forces on the client. In my experience, this is very useful as a way of clearing the air and freeing both consultant and client for real learning. It is a loaded situation, however, and not likely to succeed if done early in the life of the consultation. The stronger the client's vested interest in survival by appearing enthusiastic, the harder it will be to get a straight answer to the question of his motivation.

I believe that the most realistic approach is to assume that in the beginning phases of a consultation, clients will have a number of motives for being involved, and that these will be hard to sort out precisely, because there is a lot to lose in admitting ambivalence. As the relationship develops, trust may increase enough where it is even possible for the consultant to solve problems with a reluctant client about how to develop more positive interest in the client so that he will be more motivated to learn, or design some legitimate termination process which protects the captive client from attacks from above. Both of these are real contributions to the reluctant client.

Resistance and Resentment

When a client resists a consultant's suggestions or drags his feet about performing various kinds of follow-up activities which were supposed to have been done at a certain pace, the consultant experiences a nearly irresistible urge to blame this behavior squarely on the client's personal resistance to change. Articles are written about how to spot resistance to change, how to overcome it, and possibly someday there may be one on how to reduce it chemically.

Certainly there are clients who at times experience feelings of anxiety, frustration, fear of the consequences of an uncertain future, and the like. I believe, however, that much of the client behavior which is labeled *resistance* is really *resentment:* a feeling of anger about the process at hand; a sense that the client role as he perceives the consultant expects it to be is not satisfying or worth his time and energy. The relationship is too demeaning, the consultant is too much in control, or something else is amiss along the lines of the factors discussed in chapter eight, "Consultants and Detectives."

Locking in too early on the resistance interpretation allows the consultant to ignore the part his own behavior may be contributing to the slow progress. It also encourages the view that slow movement is the client's *individual,* internal problem.[3] The resentment hypothesis would paint the picture as a *system* issue, with its roots in either the interaction between client and consultant, or the situation in which the client finds himself in the organization.

3. The behavior of the university administrators and faculty is a classic example of this in their almost perfect tendency to account for student unrest in terms of immaturity or resistance to learning, rather than resentment of their blatantly demeaning role in the educational system.

4. Organizational Overlearning

One of the main themes of this book is the necessity to influence the process of learning if consultative activities are to have more than a passing impact on the future activities of those involved. In chapter two we examined those factors that block consultant learning. Chapter three was a consideration of several aspects of the client's role, including those which can dilute potential learning.

In this chapter, I should like to discuss an aspect of learning and change that is best observed at the level of a social system rather than at the individual level. It concerns the patterns of member learning which make it difficult for the organization to "learn" new ways of doing various activities necessary for survival in a changing environment.[1]

The phenomenon I am interested in is *organizational overlearning,* which I will simply call *Orgol.* I use the term Orgol to describe the process where members of an organization learn to do something (develop skills, increase competence, or change their world-view) and then apply this learning in unjustified ways which cause problems for the system's functioning. In these instances the problem *does not stem from a lack of learning* but rather *from an inappropriate application of learning.* Thus a potential advantage

Adapted from F. Steele, "Organizational Overlearning," *Journal of Management Studies* 9, no. 3 (October 1972), pp. 303–13. Copyright © 1972 by Basil Blackwell, Ltd.
1. Although I shall refer for convenience to organizations "learning" something, the forces obviously still reside in the members who make choices of behavior which lead to patterns of action for the system as a whole.

often turns into a mixed blessing due to inadequate decision rules about when and how to apply skills and knowledge.

An understanding of the phenomenon of Orgol can be quite helpful to a consultant. In particular, it provides a different view of the client's difficulties in trying to change a particular pattern of behavior. It is very confusing to a client to be treated as if he were not knowledgeable or knows nothing about a situation, when his view of himself is that he is applying precisely those principles which his experience has taught him should be useful. As the following discussion will show, the problem of change is really a two-step process: *unlearning old solutions and then developing more appropriate ones.*

There are probably a large number of ways in which the Orgol process can occur, but I have tried to reduce them to a few general types in order to clarify the process. The following four categories will be discussed here: *Type A,* where external skills are used inappropriately on internal needs; *Type B,* where external learning is distorted in internal applications; *Type C,* where trained blind areas result from professional education; and *Type D,* where conditions have changed, but old lessons are still held sacred. These are of course not the only examples of Orgol, nor are they as distinctly different as separate descriptions may imply.

Type A: External Skills Versus Internal Needs

The first type of Orgol is possibly the most obvious of the four, and it is this type which stimulated my original interest in Orgol. As members of a system perform its primary task (selling consumer products, moving travelers, healing patients, etcetera), they develop skills and styles of behavior which facilitate the performance of this task. Orgol occurs when the organization's members turn around and apply these same skills and styles of behavior to internal organizational issues which may require a very different type of handling.

A well-known example is the inappropriate intergroup

competition which develops internally in many systems. A system which develops high competence in competing with other systems by utilizing misleading actions, hidden information, stereotyping, and preemptive maneuvering often generates a climate of distrust not only between itself and its competitor, but between pairs of its internal subunits, such as marketing and manufacturing. This phenomenon has been recognized for some time by behavioral scientists (see Blake and Mouton 1961), and many attempts have been made to reduce inappropriate competition.

What has not been so well recognized is that this competition is simply one instance of a whole class of issues caused by inappropriate transfer of external style to internal organizational processes. An organization whose primary mode is essentially competitive will be likely to have internal competition as a process problem. Similarly, for other kinds of organizations we should be able to make predictions about what internal issues will be most potent from looking at the styles that their external tasks promote. As members develop competencies and get external feedback of success, they are encouraged to think that the same style should be applied to internal issues, since it gets results. Often this temptation will be particularly strong, because the internal issues are fuzzier and more uncomfortable. This is because they relate to individual evaluations, personal needs, complex influence processes, and long-term historical issues and power problems; and there exists therefore the view that these can be solved in the same way as selling a customer can reduce anxiety and a feeling of ambiguity.

Perhaps some examples are the most potent way of really providing a feel for the external-internal misapplication.

Type A, Example 1

A commercial airline's primary task can be described as moving people and baggage as efficiently, quickly, and safely as possible from one point to another. Time and schedules are a major commodity in this process. Airlines develop a remarkable facility for making changes in schedules and services with a minimum of delay (even if an occasional passenger sitting on his bag at LaGuardia Airport might argue the point).

I have observed that this facility may be translated internally into the same time pressures and sense of necessity for rapid change in not only schedules and services but in organizational structures as well. Major organizational changes, such as new reporting relationships or new policies, tend to be made with the same haste, as if a schedule were about to be missed. Memoranda are sent out announcing changes which upon examination turn out to require extensive preparation and training. Many months can be spent undoing the effects of that haste and lack of preparation.

I am not saying that all airlines are terrible at making changes in their internal structure, only that the nature of their task means that they will learn certain skills related to quick reaction times, and that they will have to deal with the tendency to apply those skills to internal issues which may have a very different time scale. Some members will do better at countering this tendency, others will do worse; but they will all have to deal with this congenital problem which is associated with their particular business.

Type A, Example 2

A very large consumer products firm with which I have worked has to sell a high volume in the market, and they must be flexible enough to counter competitors' changes in strategy as well as changes in consumers' tastes. As a result, members of the firm have developed high skills in altering market strategies, gathering intelligence reports, bringing out new products on short notice, and operating in ways which keep people guessing.

Once again these are very useful practices until they become applied whole hog inside the system as well. One of the effects on internal climate that these stratagems have produced is a low level of disclosure between different groups and different hierarchical levels concerning management's thinking about job changes, promotions, salaries, personal evaluations, and plans of different functional groups. Part of this could be explained as resulting from a fear of leaks to the outside world which would reduce the element of surprise in their strategies. However, the reality of that threat seemed small to me, and it appeared that the major force behind the secrecy and war-room atmosphere was the spirit built up by external strategies. Secretiveness was the name of the game, and it tended to transfer to internal operations as well.

There were many times when this internal style cut down the effectiveness of the system, particularly the ability of different groups to work interdependently based on one another's plans. Also, when people from different groups or levels met, there was very little disclosure of problems, and things were described as being fine all the time. This increased the amount of time it took to recognize a problem and develop a solution, particularly if it was a problem of internal organization having to do with structure, superior-subordinate relations, or other issues concerning process. To raise these kinds of issues would be to leave one's self open to an outflanking maneuver by someone else; and in the eyes of the company, a competent executive was supposed to plan ahead and cover all his bets.

As in the case of the airline, the company's external methods of operation had a big influence on its internal process. The war mentality and strategies led to high value being placed on people who looked good in those areas. Since people from different groups in fact saw each other more in connection with internal than with external matters, the internal issues were the major staging ground for showing their military prowess; and many managers described meetings as basically arenas for quasimilitary demonstrations to show that one was indeed executive material. It seems to me that the members needed to spend some time looking at the Orgol process they were using and examining its costs: missing information, slow response time in acting on internal issues (and in fact on external ones, since data were not widely shared), bad placement decisions made unilaterally, and the like.

Type A, Example 3

The third example of the first type of Orgol is the United States Internal Revenue Service. One of this organization's external tasks is continuous surveillance to combat possible noncompliance with tax laws. The basic climate between the IRS and the public tends to be one of mutual mistrust, as attested to by the many jokes about the IRS. The problem in terms of Orgol is that this suspicion is carried over to internal relations, on the justification that the employees can't afford to be caught in any malfeasance, and a climate of surveillance and suspicion is maintained internally as well. There is resentment of being spied upon, as well as of those (sometimes unknown) who do the spying. This generates a whole set of internal problems having to do with employees' sense of self-worth and responsibility, commitment to the system, and authority relations.

In each of the above-noted examples, the difficulties are caused not by simple incompetence, but by misplaced competence. External skills and styles are transferred on a one-to-one basis to internal issues which cannot be handled in the same way and are often worsened by this transfer.

Type B: External-Internal Distortions

Type B is related to Type A in that it also describes an instance where strategies applied to external problems become misapplied to internal issues. It differs from Type A in that whereas A was basically concerned with the *inappropriate* transfer of learning to the wrong problems, Type B is distinguished by potentially useful strategies transferred from external to internal situations which become *distorted* in the process. A skill learned in an external task could be quite useful internally, but its application to the internal system is harder to do and requires more attention.

The process may be likened to applying knowledge more rigidly to internal problems than the certainty of that knowledge warrants. My observations indicate that this rigidity occurs at least partly because internal organization problems strike closer to home, raise more anxiety, and pose more threats to individuals' organizational lives. They are also less clear as to their origin or solution than are the external task decisions a system faces; and there is evidence that pressures on a group to conform and adopt simplistic solutions increase as problems become more ambiguous.

Once again the most useful way to give the flavor of this process is through examples.

Type B, Example 1

Several colleagues have provided me with descriptions of their work with community action agencies. This type of organization has sprung up in many countries in the last ten years. One of their external tasks is the fostering of broad-based participation of residents in the decision-making and developmental activities of the community.

This external task often leads to a split within the agency itself over the issue of internal participation in decision making, with strong pressures for total participation. One consequence of this is often a very low ability to act quickly as a system, to respond to changing community problems, and to develop useful structures for different kinds of tasks.

My interpretation is that an external-internal distortion is at work. The knowledge they have gained about the useful effects of participation is useful in internal matters but not applicable on a rigid one-to-one basis. There are differences between a living-based community and a task-based organization. There are also differences between helping residents develop self-owned plans and doing the same with fellow agency workers when you also have a strong career interest in what the plans are.

Type B, Example 2

A large building and development firm has tried to differ from the ordinary developer in that executives take a strong interest in the people who will live in their products. They have a concern for the people as well as for the buildings and the mechanical systems. They feel that they have learned that concern for people is effective and productive in their work, as well as morally required.

This concern for people has also been focused inward on members of the company, with some beneficial results in terms of climate and commitment of members to the system's tasks. However, in true Orgol fashion, it has also had its negative consequences. For instance, concern for peoples' feelings is used as a reason for not leveling with one another about poor performance, rewards and penalties, and many other areas.

So far as the internal issues are concerned, the learning gets pulled out of shape and is the vehicle for avoiding direct conflicts and other uncomfortable issues. This in turn lowers the system's ability to assess its real human resources, to make conscious choices, and to have mastery over its own fate.

In both of the above-noted examples the organizations had acquired skills through external tasks which could be useful internally but were distorted in the process of transfer. This is due partly to the fact that the problems are somewhat different. It is also due to the different role stresses on a person when he is doing something for a client and when he is trying to do it for his own system. Management consultants often find that they are better able to help other systems in improving problem-solving ability than they are to help their own systems, where they are a part of the power issues, patterns of communication, and conflicts concerning allocation of resources. Knowledge would seem to be easier to apply to problems at a distance than to those in our own backyard.

Type C: Trained Blind Areas

One way that an organization learns is through the professional training of its individual members. The Type C Orgol is brought about by members being well trained in a particular discipline, profession, or functional area: so well trained, in fact, that they are systematically biased against dealing with certain kinds of organizational internal issues. They learn certain skills very well and develop world views that fit these skills, but this also implies the exclusion of other views of the world. As an illustration, let us consider the following examples.

Type C, Example 1

Leaders of religious organizations work hard training their members to be able to project images of what man *should* be and what the possibilities are if faith and good works are maintained and spread. This is, in a sense, the professional competence of their members. The problem with this is that it also trains organizational members to look at ideals rather than realities, even when real internal issues block performance or threaten survival. In religious groups with which I have worked a major problem for me was how to help them to deal with themselves as they *are;* they have difficulty discussing the problems their behaviors cause one another. Their training and personal styles tend to make them jump quickly to what they *ought* to be—to values—without working through and therefore influencing the forces that were causing the problems to begin with.

Type C, Example 2

I once worked with a legal group within a large research and development organization. This was a group of lawyers working on patents, licenses, and other legal aspects of the research process. They thought of themselves as professional lawyers and held all the traditional values of the law about professional competence, ethics, adversary proceedings, full preparation of cases in order to win them, and so on.

One of the problems with this professional training was the organizational climate it helped create for them. Their values supported seeing themselves as independent lawyers, each preparing and supporting his own cases and having little real need to collaborate with the others. The fact was, however, that they were quite interdependent in terms of areas such as budget, information retrieval, secretarial resources, influences on one another's cases through precedents, and linkages to the larger organization (which often treated them as a system).

Obviously the wishes generated by their professional training did not fit the realities of their situation, and this made them relatively incompetent at dealing with interpersonal issues or questions of internal structure. Their top management meetings were often stages for acting out the myth that they were all independent lawyers, even though in private they would tell me about the joint problems they had. They also found it very difficult to solve problems in their meetings, because their traditions taught them not to discuss a point until they were sure that they had a good case for their position (and of course not until they *had* a position). This adversary climate made any joint problem solving or mutual support very difficult. They could neither acknowledge their interdependencies nor explore an issue without leaving themselves open to unwanted influences and what they considered to be unprofessional shifts of opinion.

Although I have no firsthand data, my assumption would be that large, independent law firms would have many of the same trained blind areas and would therefore be similarly ineffective at dealing with internal organizational issues in ways which would resolve them and free the members' energy for productive work.

Type C, Example 3

Large architectural firms may have the same blind areas that I have predicted for law firms. Architects are trained to deal in a problem-solving manner with things, spaces, places, forms, and the like, and to measure their success by professional standards of excellence based on these elements. The vagaries of human behavior, social processes, and individual motivations are much fuzzier than the elements which an architect manipulates, and it is my observation that many architects tend to stay away from areas which are related to people in favor of manipulable technical problems (Steele 1968a).

Just as with the adversary process for lawyers, this tendency is trained into architects as a value, and the more members of an architectural firm internalize it, the less likely they are as a system to be able to deal openly with issues of internal process and to create fluid and supportive climates for their members. In a sense, their professional competence may have its biggest impact on creating an inability to *learn* from organizational issues, since they find them uncomfortable and throw away the data without generalizing from them or using them as the basis for further experimentation.

In examples 1, 2, and 3 of Type C Orgol there are really at least three factors working to decrease competence at dealing with internal system issues. One is the Type A Orgol based on the primary task of the system (proselytizing values; winning legal cases and/or covering all possible bases; creating things and places that are technically and aesthetically correct). A second is the Type C Orgol just discussed: a professional training that promotes blind areas as well as competence. The third has not been discussed directly but should be mentioned. It is the self-selection process, such as when people who like win-lose situations go into the law, or when those who are uncomfortable with interpersonal relationships choose architecture as a profession. This is not strictly speaking an example of Orgol, although the term could be stretched to fit it if we assume (rightly, I think) that a system "learns" partly through the members it selects and the world-views that they represent. An organization which hires only lawyers is gaining one kind of competence and is likely to be missing others at the same time.

Type D: Changed Conditions

The final example of Orgol that I will discuss here is the case where something learned the first time is no longer appropriate the second time because conditions have changed. The prototype of this is the famous experiment with the pike in the fish tank. He eats the minnows in the same tank for food. When a glass partition is introduced between him and the minnows, he crashes into it several times before his approach behavior is extinguished. After he stops bashing his nose, the glass is removed, and the minnows swim undisturbed on their side of the tank. The pike will starve even though food is available because he has "learned" that all he will get for his trouble is a sore nose. When the glass was removed, the conditions were changed, but his view of them did not. This is clearly a case of overlearning, where a lesson was then taken as a given and is no longer tested for validity.

In my experience, this is a very widespread phenomenon in organizational life, and it occurs on both external and internal issues. On the external task, Perlo provides a nice illustration.

> But it is common knowledge that Douglas' losses then, like Lockheed's and General Dynamics' huge losses a few years earlier, were in civilian planes. If one may generalize, they all tried to get away with the same grossly wasteful practices that paid off in military business. Similarly, Mr. Ling's operation is in the deep red because the methods which worked in the Texan's defense production lost hundreds of millions when tried on his steel industry acquisition, Jones and Laughlin. [Perlo, 1970]

On the internal side, organizational structures that do not work successfully at one stage of a system's growth are then assumed to be bad alternatives; even when later stages of development will make them very appropriate. Conversely, a structure which solves a particular problem or works during a stage of the system's life is grasped and hung onto long beyond its real usefulness.

There are many reasons why lessons learned at one point are not tested for their continuing relevance to the present and future. One is the members' wish for it not to appear as though a "mistake" had been made in the past. This aversion can make it difficult to raise the question of whether old truths still hold. The converse would be an organization which ascribed to the idea that any solution could be good for its time but will be likely to decrease in relevance over time, and that this is a natural process, not a crisis. Systems which are most susceptible to Orgol may be those which search for permanent, all-around solutions to necessarily fluid problems.

Another force which inhibits relearning is the internal evaluation game in organizations. The more career cost there is to having one's name associated with a solution now found to be inadequate (even if it was excellent when the decision was made), the more people will resist reexamining their own lessons and dropping old structures. This is more true the less subordinates trust the competence of superiors to put subordinates' decisions in the context of the time and place in which they were made.

This suggests another force against examining assumptions. As I have pointed out in an earlier article, not only do people not test for whether conditions have changed, they often were not even aware of what the context and conditions of the original "lesson" were (Steele 1968 b). The more concrete and literal the thinking of those drawing the conclusions, the more likely they are to generalize far beyond the specific limitations of time and setting.

Finally, another evaluative process blocks solutions, lessons, and conditions from being reexamined for current relevance. Many bosses (and peers) censure members for raising issues on which decisions have already been made by the boss, particularly if the area is taboo or one around which there was a good deal of conflict. Anyone who raises this kind of issue again runs the risk of being labeled negative, overpersevering, or simply a troublemaker who is not pulling with the team.

In essence, these cases represent an instance where the boss cannot discriminate between an attempt at gaining influence (which he automatically assumes it to be) and a process for testing information (which is what the subordinate may intend). If the cost of reexamining old solutions or assumptions is high, then the systems will be slow to sense when old learning is no longer valued.

FIG. 2. *"I could have a gold mine here if I could only enlarge the place."* Drawing by Starke; © 1969 The New Yorker Magazine, Inc.

In a sense, the forces in our society challenging the military-industrial complex and the environmental crisis represent the struggle to develop a more acceptable testing process. Loren Eiseley posed this as a challenge to all mankind when he wrote:

The need is not really for more brains,
the need is now for a gentler, a more tolerant people
than those who won for us
against the ice, the tiger, and the bear.

[1967, p. 13]

Conclusions

To summarize briefly, organizational members engage in learning or develop styles which are both strengths and potential weaknesses. While developing an identity or competency they may also be building in a blind or congenital problem area, usually in terms of their ability to deal with internal issues. (But this may not always be so. Witness Starke's wonderful cartoon about the innkeeper with a congenital problem built into his business's identity, in figure 2.)

Four types of overlearning have been touched on here, and each raises a particular diagnostic question. For Type A, it is, What internal process issues are likely to be fostered by the system's competence at the primary task? For Type B, What types of distortions are likely to occur in the application of external skills to fuzzier internal problems? For Type C, What trained incompetencies or blind areas due to professional training are likely to reduce the system's effectiveness? For Type D there are two questions: Were lessons which the organization learned generalized from a sufficiently specific view of the conditions which led to the consequences? and Does the system have internal forces working which tend to keep members from testing for changes in conditions or problem demands? That is, are the lessons still valid?

One function of the concept of Orgol as it has been sketched here is that it has helped me to understand a phenomenon that I have observed often and with some curiosity: an organization which has experienced great success in providing a service to clients does relatively poorly when it provides those services inside the system. Doing an external task and dealing with internal issues have different pressures and role stresses, even when they are in the same area of expertise.

Similarly, in my work as a behavioral science consultant, the concept of Orgol has been a useful tool for clues as to where change processes can be supported in a system. It seems to me a truism that most people do not *try* to be ineffective; most of them have what Buhler has called "constructive intent" (1962). In order to change behavior, it is quite useful to understand what the actors feel is the *function of the present behavior,* that is, what lessons are they or the system continuing to act out, and under what conditions were these learned? These questions can suggest very practical strategies for facilitating new learning.

The processes of differentiation and generalization of knowledge are both very important for any human organization. To reduce the costs of Orgol, an organization's members need to develop complex rules of decision as to when and how to apply various skills, styles, and knowledge. One example of this would be Argyris's proposal for different structures for different classes of decisions within an organization (1964).

Even more directly applicable to Orgol problems is the issue of what kinds of skills and styles of behavior are rewarded by the power centers of the organization. The implication of this discussion is that in a healthy organization there is value placed on a multiplicity of skills and approaches. Without this, the system's members will be unable or unwilling to deal with certain problems, particularly those related to internal organization processes. In systems where sales, engineering, production, or whatever have become *the* single source of all wisdom, members will not be able to muster enough real wisdom (or it will not be listened to) to deal with their process issues under changing conditions.

Organizational members who wish to learn and to continually renew their systems must promote a climate where there is support for raising issues, testing old assumptions about learning that may no longer be relevant, and examining the consequences of actions without seeking scapegoats to receive the blame for changing conditions. If this climate can be promoted, the members are well on their way to avoiding both underlearning, which has traditionally been accepted as an evil, and overlearning, which has generally been either overlooked or praised as consistency.

5. Using the Laboratory Method to Train Consultants and Clients

The laboratory training method for learning about behavior is approximately twenty-seven years of age.[1] During this first phase of its use, its most famous form, the T-group, or encounter group, was thought by many to be a miracle solution to their personal, interpersonal, or organization problems. I think it is safe to say, however, that the honeymoon is now over. More and more articles appear which speak of the drawbacks as well as the advantages of T-group and other laboratory experiences. Organizations which have used laboratory methods consistently are now attempting to be more selective, using them when they fit a larger design for systematic organizational development.

In this chapter I will discuss a particular application of laboratory training which I do *not* think is outdated: its use in training consultants and clients who are involved in planned change projects. I believe that the nature of the consulting process today makes the laboratory method of training more relevant than ever. I will be illustrating the ways in which the laboratory method, in comparison with more didactic teaching methods, tends to provide more opportunities for concrete practice of roles; to provide generalized learning about issues which can be applied to a range of

A shorter version of this chapter appeared under the same title in *Training and Development Journal* 23, no. 6 (June 1969), pp. 10–16. Reproduced by special permission from *Training and Development Journal*. Copyright 1969 by the American Society for Training and Development, Inc.

1. For a history of the first seventeen years, see Bradford, Gibb, and Benne (1964).

specific problem situations; and to provide learning situations where a person can choose an action for himself, get feedback about the results, and make his own generalizations, thereby increasing his sense of competence at the process of learning itself. I will say more about the laboratory method after a brief look at consulting.

The Role of Consulting Today

What is the nature of consulting today? To review chapter one briefly, one component is a shift in the conception of change from something that must be avoided or neutralized to something that is inevitable and represents one of the basic environmental features with which any human system must learn to deal competently. More and more organizations are becoming aware of the fact that their survival and healthy growth depend on their ability to diagnose changing needs, to perceive potential resources, and to invent the necessary steps which will bring the two together.

Along with this shift in the conception of change from an unusual situation of crisis to a regular, natural part of a system's healthy life, there has emerged a shift in the conception of the role of the consultant. Consulting traditionally had meant functioning as an expert who, when called in to solve some specific organizational problem or crisis, collected data and provided the solution for the client's system. There is a trend, at least in behavioral-social system change efforts, away from a *content*-oriented "expert" consulting role and toward a *process*-oriented, "facilitator" role aimed at helping the organization develop its own built-in competencies for continuing change and development. Schein has written a full-length book specifically about process consultation (1969), while Argyris has also done an invaluable job of thinking and writing about the longer-term process conception of change (1970).

This and other recent work also makes it clear that the consultant's role is no longer necessarily played by someone outside the system. In this chapter, the term *consultant* is meant to apply to both external and internal agents of change; the defining characteristic is simply that a person in a consulting role sees as his primary responsibility the facilitation of change in the system's procedures, climate, policies, problem-solving processes, et cetera, rather than having primary responsibility for the content of any of the organization's external (such as marketing) or internal (such as accounting) tasks.

Whether external or internal, the consultant as he is developing today has a need for a somewhat different set of competencies than those required in the past. Rather than being called upon to be knowledgeable only in content areas such as organizational structure, finance, or general management practices, this new consultant needs to be aware of current theories of organization, to be aware of his own needs and styles, to be skilled in diagnosing resistances to change, to create appropriate learning conditions for different problem areas and personal styles of different clients, and to be able to confront conflicts between himself and the client in a constructive manner. This is a much more demanding role, and the processes required for developing process skills are presumably different or at least more complex than simply learning the content of behavioral science and management theories.

If you accept these demands as being realistic today, then it follows that those who are engaged in the process of developing this new style of change activity have a responsibility also to concern themselves with how process-oriented change consultants are trained or developed. We need to concern ourselves with developing theories and gathering data about learning processes relevant to these role behaviors. To my knowledge, very little has, in fact, been put down in accessible form to date.[2] I hope that this chapter will help to fill the gap, and that it will spur others to explore consultant training. As a vehicle for doing this, I will, in the remainder

2. For me, the most useful work so far has been the volume by Truax and Carkhuff on the training of psychotherapists (1968). They show the importance of personal experience to learning in areas such as empathy which combine emotions and intellect as influences on the therapist's behavior.

of this chapter, discuss primarily my own observations and experience with one device for training consultants: staff work in the T-group and in related laboratory designs for learning. I will also be discussing the T-group's use as a means of training *clients* as well. Conceptualizations of work on training clients how to fulfill their own roles in the process of receiving help have been in even shorter supply than those on the training of consultants.

The Laboratory Training Process

When I refer to the T-group or to the laboratory method here, I mean a behaviorally oriented learning setting which creates immediate social dilemmas which provide opportunities for action for the participants and staff. These actions are used as the major data inputs for learning. A number of features of the laboratory method T-group are relevant to our purposes. One is that the learner usually has primary responsibility for his own involvement, behavior, and learning. In the T-group in particular, there is a face-to-face situation where people can act and give and get reactions with a relatively efficient use of communication energy (for example, they do not send memos and wait a week for replies). Another important aspect of the laboratory method is the fact that social groupings are there by design. The group has reasons (usually learning, although individual goals may vary widely) for existence. It is not accidental. It is bounded by time; it has a starting point and life span, usually specified in advance and quite limited (a weekend, a week, two weeks). And it has a certain membership, also usually specified. Finally, I have described the laboratory method elsewhere as "reality training": learning how to use data in an immediate situation in order to learn from our real (not distorted) day-to-day experiences (Steele 1968*b*).

In essence, this view is similar to Slater's conceptualization of the T-group as a "microcosm" of a larger system or society (1961). The group deals with many themes that a larger system goes through in more extended (and often less visible) ways: the birth, existence, and death of the system;

the survival of the system and its members; issues of control, conformity, deviance, value differences; and so on. The members create a culture, through both conscious and unconscious choices, which has dynamic qualities similar to many of the systems in which they live and work from day to day.

A staff member (or *trainer*) who works with such a group is essentially a consultant[3] to a system which has norms, values, roles, increasing differentiation and specialization, and other attributes which can be examined and influenced. As such, he can obtain information about himself and his responses in that role, about the dynamics between him and the group, about change and different forms of resistance to change, and about the problems of collaboration and dependency. The more self-aware the trainer is of his role in the group, the more likely he is to learn things that can be generalized to apply to his work with other client systems.

Positive Features of the T-Group for Consultant-Training

In order to be more specific about this learning process, what are some of the features of the T-group setting which make it valuable and facilitate transfer of learning by the trainer to a more general consulting role? One feature is the *compressed time sequence* of the typical laboratory session. Things happen at a faster pace than during the usual organization routine. This allows a trainer to act and to get relatively immediate feedback on the consequences of his intervention. In an organization, this kind of feedback often occurs over weeks or months and is much harder to connect with the consultant's specific behaviors. Observing a T-group transaction is a little like using time-lapse photography to observe flower growth rather than sitting in a garden all spring. Besides seeing a wider range of behaviors in a shorter time, it also takes considerably less energy to get feedback

3. In fact, the Tavistock wing of the training field calls the staff member *the consultant*.

on the impact of an intervention. Of course, this time span varies with the nature of the intervention and the state of the group at a given time. In the T-group there are still situations when the time lag or the impact of an intervention is such that it is hard to tie in with the original act.

A second feature of the T-group is simply the fact that the trainer must make *choices of action* in a context where people who are interacting with him look to him (either overtly or covertly) for some kind of guidance about appropriate behaviors. The participants tend to look to him for leadership. He may choose *not* to act in a given situation, but this is in itself a choice of action like any other. This is a realistic alternative in terms of the kinds of dilemmas he would face as a consultant in an organization.

Third, the T-group provides a *temporary system* where structural and other kinds of changes can be instituted for limited periods of time with relatively small inputs of energy and commitment compared to that which must be expended in an actual organization. This means that it is possible to experiment with new forms or with new ways of intervening in a much more economical way than it is in a total system. Similarly, data about effects can be collected more quickly.

Still another feature of the T-group which makes it good for consultant training purposes is the fact that it is a setting which legitimizes *discussing the reciprocal roles of the trainer and the participants*. Signals indicate that it is all right to look at goals, behaviors, and personal styles, including those of the trainer.[4] The effective T-group setting creates a freer climate for interchanges of this kind. Of course, one goal of a real consultant-client relationship is also to establish this open climate; but given the broader forces of the history and norms of the organization, it usually takes considerably longer and may be a less intense interaction than that established in the laboratory.

4. Although staff members vary in their willingness to throw themselves into this. The obvious implication here is that a trainer loses an opportunity to learn about his consulting style if he defines his own behavior as an illegitimate topic.

A useful aspect of the T-group that is often overlooked is its *manageable scale*. Real issues, such as conflicting expectations of roles, tend to occur on a scale that can be understood without long study. The data are there to be seen; peoples' reactions can be observed, since they are in the same place; and the staff and other participants are there to see them. This means that it is possible to get some understanding of and generalize about issues which would be less visible in a complex organization. This manageable scale also has some drawbacks, which will be discussed later.

Finally, the T-group also provides the opportunity for *practice in collaboration* with other staff in the process of intervention. The experience of cotraining has much in it that can be transferred to teamwork in broader consultation. There are problems connected with different personal styles of the trainers. There are choices to be made about how issues between the trainers are handled (on what level, openly within the group or in private, et cetera). There are effects of these choices on the process of change, and there are valuable data that each staff member has as potential feedback for the other which can be filed away or shared in a common learning experience.[5] I see all of these elements as quite relevant to the consulting process, and T-group work may help a consultant to accept these issues as part of the role, rather than feel that they are threats to be avoided. To the extent that there is this acceptance, the consultative process will be a growing, changing, instructive one for the consultant as well as for the client (and in fact *unless* it is that for the consultant, it may not be one for the client in the long run).

Given the above-noted ways in which T-group staff work experience can be generalized to a broader consultant role, it is no historical accident that many of the newer breed of process-oriented consultants have moved into consulting from beginnings as group workers and T-group trainers. I would expect this trend to continue until there are sufficient alternative training grounds.

5. For a discussion of these issues, see chapter seven on consulting teamwork.

Using the T-Group for Training Clients

Many organizational consultants today recommend that their clients attend some form of laboratory training. The reasons given for this usually relate to learning how to deal better with others, how to solve problems about behavioral issues, and so on. These are important outcomes, but I believe that clients are sent to laboratories for another reason, one which is often not appreciated even by the consultant: he is sent to be trained *how to be a good client*. I believe that this is the most important single outcome from organizational members attending a laboratory session; they learn how to play a client's role in relation to the consultant.

How does this kind of learning occur in the T-group? For one, it provides concrete experiences for the T-group member in receiving help, both from the trainer and from other group members. He functions in a setting where he can unashamedly look at his own reactions to being helped or not helped. He can observe the extent to which he looks to the trainer for various kinds of expertise, especially in situations where he should be providing it himself. The group setting also legitimizes getting data from others and from the trainer about themselves as learners and their degrees of comfort or discomfort in that particular role.

More generally, the T-group member who will be a client can explore some of the necessary conditions for change and do this in the context of manageable changes, namely, changes in the structure or process of the immediate group as it is functioning over a short period of time within a limited framework. For instance, he may feel and recognize within himself resistance to changing something as simple as the seating arrangement or the level of lighting in the group room. The T-group, it seems to me, provides very nice data for resistance to change in terms of both an individual level and a group system level. These resistances are so evident at various points in the life of the group that they become the central learning focus in many laboratory situations. Experiencing these blocks or resistances and seeing how much energy it takes to work them through can be a very eye-opening experience for a participant, helping him to see how much work he has to do as a client if he is to facilitate changes in his own organization.

In addition to learning about specific change issues, it often happens that a participant in a T-group develops a greater feeling for the legitimacy of the organizational consulting process. This is especially helpful in clarifying the point that it is not necessarily a failure or a sickness to ask someone to provide help from the outside. I think that the notion of help in technical matters (research, accounting, or information processing) still is more acceptable as a natural part of the growth of a healthy system with limited internal resources than that of the reception of help in organizational and social processes. Managers and administrators in many different kinds of organizations feel that they should be "experts" on people. This feeling can be opened up and explored in the laboratory training process.

A client also needs some specific skills to perform his role. In the T-group he learns observational and descriptive skills that essentially provide him with a behavioral *language* that he can use in working with a consultant. This language may be the most important concrete learning that a laboratory participant could take home with him. It provides a base for further learning about self, for sharing some new ideas with others, and for working with behavioral science consultants in his organization. The T-group also legitimizes using this new language where it makes the most difference: in discussing the here and now, and in the immediate experiences shared by client and consultant.

In essence, the T-group provides a setting where trainer and group work out what the client-consultant relationship will be like in that given instance; and in the process, many rich data are produced about this particular issue for other consultation processes. This will generally be less true, however, the more a trainer has a particular set program for how he ought to behave in that role. The more specifically he has his style or relationship with the participants programmed in advance, the less he and they are likely to learn about the process of developing a consultant-client relationship in a more unknown system.

Finally, it is interesting to note that Malamud and Machover (1965) have developed a set of psychological group exercises which were designed in response to a need very similar to the one postulated here. Just as I believe clients need role development, Malamud and Machover believe that patients in therapy need to learn the role and skills of being patients. Their exercises are designed for use *before* a person goes into therapy, on the assumption that he starts out ahead of the game if he is comfortable with psychological terms, with introspection, and with looking at behavior in descriptive rather than evaluative terms. For an organizational client, a good T-group experience provides much the same kind of learning and preparation.

Main Features of the T-Group

The various conditions which have been described in the two previous sections fall under two very general categories: the advantages of a manageable *scale,* and the advantages derived from *norms which legitimize behaviors* which are likely to lead to learning. These conditions, in turn, lead to two major consequences which account for the potency of the T-group as an educational setting for the consultant's and client's role performances. One is that there are opportunities for live, real *role practice* where giving and receiving help, attempts at changing the system, and other experiments can be tried in the natural course of the program. The second is that more *information* is available about the effects, difficulties, and complications of that practice, so that it is possible to learn from them. These features are summarized in figure 3.

Note also that these consequences are not so discreet and independent as they are shown in the figure. For instance, one of the kinds of practice that is so important in the laboratory is that of providing more information to others than we usually do: letting them know what we saw or felt at a given moment rather than keeping this to ourselves. This, in turn, is the process whereby the legitimizing norms really

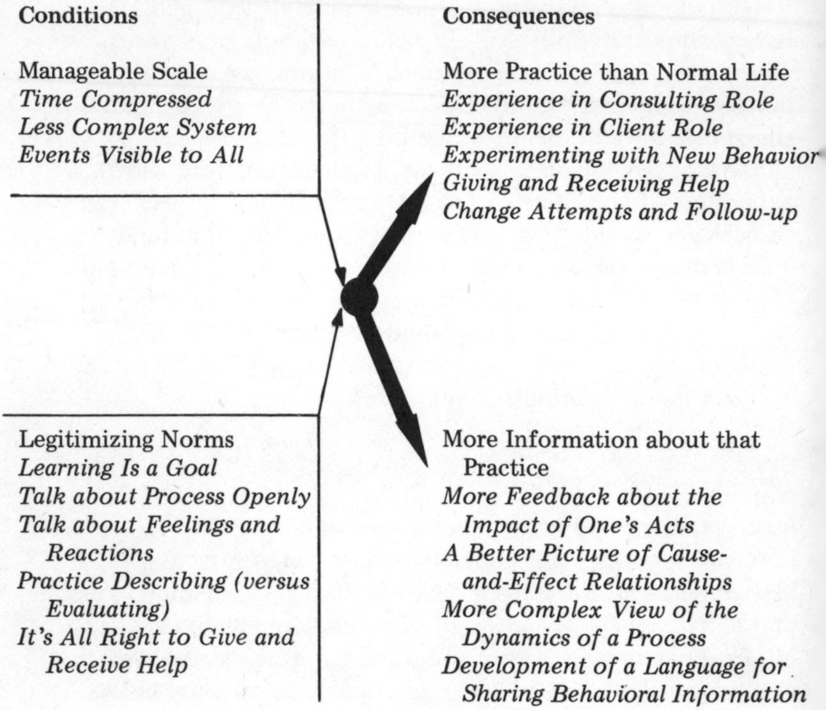

Conditions	Consequences
Manageable Scale	More Practice than Normal Life
Time Compressed	*Experience in Consulting Role*
Less Complex System	*Experience in Client Role*
Events Visible to All	*Experimenting with New Behavior*
	Giving and Receiving Help
	Change Attempts and Follow-up

Legitimizing Norms	More Information about that
Learning Is a Goal	Practice
Talk about Process Openly	*More Feedback about the*
Talk about Feelings and	*Impact of One's Acts*
Reactions	*A Better Picture of Cause-*
Practice Describing (versus	*and-Effect Relationships*
Evaluating)	*More Complex View of the*
It's All Right to Give and	*Dynamics of a Process*
Receive Help	*Development of a Language for*
	Sharing Behavioral Information

FIG. 3. Attributes of the T-Group for Consultant-Client Learning

develop effectively. The trainer and the beginning setting (including peoples' expectations) get the process started, but it really flowers only if people *do* begin to practice some new behaviors and build a sense of trust in the group as a place where one can experiment. Groups which develop this circular process of (Legitimation——→experimentation——→ sharing——→legitimation) will tend to produce good consultants and clients. Those which do not will tend to produce experiences for their members which the members then try to "do" for someone else, like passing on a bag of candy. This is not likely to be effective training for consultants or clients.

Limitations of the T-Group

Besides whether or not the particular group develops well, there are several structural features of the T-group situation which have a negative effect on learning about consulting in live organizations. One of these limitations is the reverse of the benefits of the compressed time scale. This compression also gives a limited time perspective to peoples' expectations and behaviors. The group is usually without a history and has no expected future life. The short time perspective removes certain very strong realities that exist in most organizations (such as memories of departed souls). This makes it harder to use the small group to learn about long-term organizational issues. The same limitation also holds for certain aspects of power, at least in the T-group of strangers, and it is hard to develop through the small group the degree of understanding of complex organizational reward systems which can be developed by working with an actual live organization.

In general, one of the T-group's strengths, its face-to-face quality, also is its limitation where learning about organizational processes is concerned. Sometimes it is very difficult to generalize from this experience of face-to-face communication to a very complex or structurally and historically rooted organizational problem with many things happening in unobservable and undefinable ways.

In addition, work in the T-group can also provide clients and consultants with mislearning at certain points. For instance, the consultant may learn through T-group work that the T-group is *the* answer, so far as intervention in the organization is concerned, to almost any kind of problem or issue. I have also known of consultants who believed that all situations having to do with change in organizations are really T-groups in disguise and have the same dynamics. In fact, at any given time the relevant strategies, goals, and structural problems may be quite unrelated to a face-to-face interpersonal process.

From a client's point of view, there are several instances of mislearning which he may come away with. One is that he may define his trainer as what a consultant "ought" to be like, which clearly misses the variability and range of styles which are possible for different change agents and are appropriate given different problematic situations in the organization. I have seen many T-group participants find it very difficult to accept as a consultant a person who behaved in a way that was different from the behavior of the first trainer they had encountered.

A second mislearning which the client may carry away from a laboratory is the message that the T-group is what an organization ought to be like all the time. This clearly leads to problems when there are different kinds of tasks, different work groups, different demands made by the organization, and different kinds of relationships that must be formed. Some of these situations can be quite like a T-group, and some should bear very little resemblance to the low task demands of the T-group. The problem is that the laboratory learning method becomes regarded as a cure-all rather than as literally a means for learning.

Transfer of Learning: Personality

In order to adequately analyze the laboratory method as a learning situation for training in the roles of consultant and client, we must consider the two major factors that determine transfer of learning from one situation to another: the nature of the situations (similarities, degree of threat in each, et cetera) and the personality of the learner involved. Space does not permit dealing in depth with the personality question here; but before presenting some situational concepts, I would like to suggest in passing the kinds of personality dimensions that I think affect transfer of learning from the laboratory setting to the organization.[6]

One important variable is the level of basic nondefensiveness (tendency to attend to immediate experience accurately whether or not it fits one's present self-image) versus the tendency to repress or distort disliked data. In order to learn accurately, the laboratory trainer or participant has to allow the data to come into his system so that they can be used. He needs to possess a minimum level of self-acceptance as an imperfect, changing, learning human being. A second dimension is what has generally been called cognitive complexity, or the ability to think abstractly (Harvey, Hunt, and Schroder 1961) and to develop complex rules for combining data from different dimensions into propositions about cause and effect (Schroder, Driver and Streufert 1967). Without these abilities, a learner is usually most aware of feelings of discomfort, ambiguity, and a lack of relevance to the real world as he experiences a laboratory program.

Finally, learning from immediate experience is influenced by one's style in perceiving the world: not *how much* one perceives undistorted, or how one *combines* these data, but *what kinds of data* a person can perceive. My basic assumption is that a learner in a laboratory session needs to be able to tune in to internal, self-generated data which are his own feelings as well as to the information collected about the outside world through his five senses. This tuning in to internal data is what Jung called operating with "intuition" (see Myers 1962) as well as sensation. Intuition is essential in generating contextual propositions about the relevance of data from the present situation and transferring learning appropriately to other situations which do not have a one-to-one correspondence to the learning situation. This process sug-

6. For a research report on personality factors as an influence on laboratory learning, see Steele (1968*b*).

gests that a training laboratory has data which are more useful for learning about dilemmas or issues than learning specific rules about what "should" be done in all cases. Those who have the ability to look at an event and say, "I have learned about the major forces on me in this kind of situation, so I can gather data about this dilemma or choice in other places, like my home organization," are likely to become more effective consultants or clients through laboratory training. Those who say to themselves, "I've learned never to say *that* in a group again," are oriented toward learning straight rules which they can apply completely. The latter type of person learns little of real process value from a laboratory.

Transfer of Learning: The Situation

Returning to the situation as a determinant of transferable learning about consulting and change, we have focused our attention primarily on the basic T-group setting. But the laboratory method is much broader than the T-group and encompasses any kind of activity which generates behavioral data and legitimizes processing these data for learning purposes. From what has been said above, it seems obvious that learning for consultants and clients is enhanced by providing more kinds of role-connected experiences in a laboratory, where they can practice dealing with relevant process issues. There are many effective laboratory exercises already in use today:intergroup exercises, trust-formation and bargaining games, communication (one-way and two-way) exercises, and so on. Behind them is the basic assumption that it is possible to invent specific situations which maximize the learning which will be generalized to nonlaboratory settings.

This assumption really is a statement of the underlying theme of this chapter. If possible, these laboratory experiences should have the advantages of manageable scale and legitimation of learning which were discussed above and should overcome the disadvantage (of the T-group) of lack of more complex organizational phenomena. In the remainder of the chapter I will describe briefly three laboratories which I think have these qualities and provide excellent settings for learning about change: the organization laboratory, the laboratory in autonomy, initiative, and risk-taking, and the live laboratory consultation.

The organization laboratory. In the organization laboratory, the main purpose is to learn about organizational dynamics and how they may be influenced. The design is usually to form an organization out of the total laboratory population. Sometimes the exercise is structured to resemble the form of the organization, its primary task, rules for relating to the environment, and so on. The most historically interesting type of organization laboratory is that described by Harvey, Oshry, and Watson (1970), where no preconditions are set down other than that the laboratory is to form a purposive human organization, and that there are certain facilities available such as library and meeting spaces. The essential requirements of the design are only that participants (including staff, who have to find their own roles to play just as other members do) be trying to learn from the process; that there be a minimum length of time for the system to develop (three to four days is probably minimum); and that there be enough people so that the system cannot function effectively as one large, face-to-face group (Harvey, Oshry and Watson suggest twenty-seven participants as a bare minimum). This last requirement is to build in more complexity than the T-group's setting contains.

As people go through the process of forming and developing the organization and operating it, many dynamics are created which are quite similar to the organizations back home. It is possible if you work hard at it to draw some very significant organization-level learning from the process. For example, in a number of exercises in which I have participated, staff groups have been formed which almost universally take themselves out of the action fairly early in the exercise to do their planning and work with themselves as a staff group and thereby lose touch with the organization and what it is doing. In three different organization laboratories I have seen self-styled staff units plan (in isolation) activities which they think will help the organization. When they come back to the organization to propose it, they generally find to their surprise that conditions have changed, and their plans are no longer relevant. Another example of a real-life dynamic is the degree of top-heaviness, or "management lump," as compared to the actual productive force, which tends to be created in the organization. In one exercise for a religious group, approximately 70 percent of the members of the organization of thirty-six persons was made up of either management or staff, with 28 percent actually turning out the product which was the main task of the organization.

Often the training staff has a very difficult time intervening in the organization and helping it to learn about itself as it goes along. I cannot think of a more realistic issue for a learning consultant to have to deal with than on-line processing, since it is an issue that every consultant faces, either explicitly or implicitly. As Harvey, Oshry, and Watson describe this dilemma for the free organization laboratory, it tends to be very explicit and generate anxieties in the staff:

> Since the process and outcome of the laboratory are unsure, the roles of individual staff members may be quite different from the roles they play in more traditional sensitivity training laboratories. For example, in more traditional designs, staff members have certain prerogatives and authority as a function of their staff roles. They "run" T-groups, set the schedule, design structured activities, and, in general, organize the community. In brief, they are "line managers."
>
> In this design, where the role of staff is far less clear, the definition of that role depends greatly on how each individual staff member can gain a foothold in the organization as it takes shape. Some may turn out to be trainers, some consultants, some line managers, some workers, and some left out. [1970, p. 409]

The point is that this process of working out a viable role and relationship as consultant to a system is a vital and difficult part of consulting. The straight T-group trainer role is now so well defined that it does not carry the uncertainty necessary for learning about this role-definition process, whereas serving as a staff member in one of these free organization laboratories requires that staff and participants alike practice the process of definition of self and role.

This openness also provides opportunities for participants as well as staff to serve in consulting functions. Harvey, Oshry, and Watson describe an episode where members of the Experience-based Learning group (low structure) design an exercise in which they serve as process consultants for the Seminar group. It is harder for participants to achieve real consulting experiences in the traditional T-group, where the trainer tends to become certified as the only real "expert" in the crowd.[7]

The laboratory organization's members, on the other hand, often learn about the kinds of resentment and anger they feel towards the helpers in the exercise (and toward consultants in their home organizations when they are "interrupted" in the flow of getting something done with tight time constraints). The lab exercise helps them to see themselves as pushing away help when they most need it. They sometimes see that they may be actually adding to the time it takes them to do a task and lowering the quality of the output by simply getting something out which they think they have time to do only without interruption from anybody else. The clients also get an opportunity to see that the time when they may be *least* able to use outside help is when they are having internal problems, just the time when they *most* need it. They often recognize that it would take some very conscious diagnosis and willingness to deal in the open with those feelings of resentment or rejection in order to get past that bogged-down point and move to a new level of collaboration with consultants or other people who might be of service to them.

To my knowledge, the development with the most impact in the organization laboratory is the NTL Institute's Power and Systems Laboratory, which I have helped Barry Oshry de-

7. Especially when many participants bring with them the traditional view of consulting practice or, rather, of their view of their role as client, which means that they are to be advised by an expert on some content issue.

velop over the past three years. The laboratory consists of a live system in which all who attend participate for three to four days and spend the following two days analyzing the experience. Power and resource differentials are built into the beginning structure, and everything is a part of the lab's system, including the sleeping and eating arrangements and control of money and luggage. The experience is very compelling and provides a rich setting in which both consultants and clients can learn about power, influence, and various social forces which promote stability and change in organizations.

The laboratory in autonomy, initiative, and risk-taking. The autonomy laboratory has been developed primarily by Roger Harrison. The core of its design is the provision of a rich and responsive environment which has reading materials, games, diagnostic instruments, electronic equipment, varied meeting spaces, a mixture of participants and participant skills, and a number of staff members. There is no set schedule for the day's activities, so that first and foremost the participant is confronted with questions such as, Why have I come here? What are my high priority learning areas? What materials do I need in order to learn in these areas? How do I acquire these resources and get started? How am I doing in terms of my ability to control my own learning process?

As the autonomy laboratory progresses, staff members play two major roles: as resources for whatever interests the participants may have, and as facilitators of participants' examination of their self-directed learning process and the blocks to it. In the latter area, I regularly use the blocks to learning dimensions described in chapter two of this book.

This laboratory is particularly useful to people whose work roles require that they be able to function with few guidelines, undefined responsibilities, and multiple possibilities for use of time and energy. I believe that this describes the demands of the consultant's role very well, and the autonomy laboratory is thus an excellent consultant training experience. It also has worked well for people (potential clients) in regular organizational roles which have loose or changing guidelines and scope for influencing others without necessarily being in a formal position of power.

The live lab consultation. The live laboratory consultation is an example of laboratory-based consultant training that has grown out of several NTL Institute programs, especially the consulting skills laboratory and the program for specialists in organization development. For convenience I will refer to it as the live lab consultation, or LLC. This simply means that in a laboratory designed specifically for consultant training, there is built into it a consultation project serving a real client system. Its time scale depends on the length of the program, but essentially the LLC is a short-term, compressed consulting experience with some client in the area (for convenience's sake), where there are real problems of definition of goals, relationship formation, data collection, use of data, intervention strategies, team relations, termination, and evaluation of results. The rest of the laboratory is built around the projects and serves as a vehicle for inputs of theory, discussion of specific problems that the consultants (who usually work in teams) are experiencing, and processing of experiences to generalize and share learning.

The basic assumptions of the LLC are that (1) actual concrete role experience is most likely to generate a sense of involvement and a commitment to taking action; and that (2) this action can be used for learning if it occurs in the supportive context of a training laboratory where the process of learning is strongly legitimized. In this regard, it is a direct extension of the argument developed in this chapter. The use of the LLC really began when we realized that the boundaries of the usual laboratory had been arbitrarily limited.[8] It became clearer to us that the community surrounding a particular program was a natural laboratory in itself, and that it contained many potential client systems which would welcome being involved in a dynamic learning pro-

8. I say we, because many people, unfortunately too numerous to mention here, have been involved in the development of the LLC.

cess. This has been our experience to date, and the consulting projects have generally been stimulating to both the clients and the consulting teams.

I should add that this is not an easy laboratory with which to work. The projects become very involving, and inventive designs are needed to keep the forces I described in chapter two from driving out processing and other learning activities because of anxiety about performance. The projects develop a very powerful life of their own, and teams become invested in them. This means that it is also likely that competitive feelings will develop over who is doing the "best" project, and these feelings will have to be dealt with if sharing of experiences and useful confrontations are to occur. Far from being irrelevant to the task at hand, however, even these process problems in the LLC are useful if looked at openly (and shared with the participants), since they represent live examples of the issue of how consultants, especially in teams, learn from their experiences rather than just undergoing them. The LLC is a concrete means of dealing with many of the issues of learning that were discussed earlier, since it generates them in a clear manner.

A Brief Summary

Several strands have wound their way through this chapter. One is that consultation as a profession is becoming more concerned with *process* issues: both how the client's process of interaction helps or hinders task performance, and how the process of change itself can be facilitated by consultant action. Second, the T-group, through being compressed in scale and creating an atmosphere which legitimates self-examination and observation, provides both trainers and participants with sharpened views of dynamics which are occurring in less visible ways in more complex systems. Third, a particular kind of stance is needed by the trainer and by the participant in order to learn about the consultant-client process; a stance including self-acceptance, dealing with complexity and fuzziness, and a willingness to look for and accept the limitations to the kind of generalizations that can be taken from an event and its consequences.

Finally, the T-group has limitations as a device for learning about organizational change, and it should be thought of as only one example of use of the laboratory method of generating live data which can be processed for both cognitive and emotional learning purposes. Three examples were given: the organization laboratory, the laboratory in autonomy, initiative, and risk-taking, and the live laboratory consultation. I am sure that many other laboratory designs will be developed to meet specific learning goals related to participation in planned efforts of change by clients and consultants.

In closing, let me ask once again the question, Why use the laboratory method for consultant-client training rather than more didactic methods? I think this chapter has suggested several answers to this question. For one, the laboratory method generates a higher motivation to learn, since it provides role practice that makes the participant *feel* the need to understand particular issues better. He is not simply told that feelings of resentment get in the way of receiving help, he experiences this and tries to learn about it when those feelings are fairly current. For another, the laboratory method models a learning process which is likely to be more effective than didactic learning in the context of consultants' and clients' day-to-day experiences. The great bulk of their learning depends on how well they use these experiences, not on how many lectures or courses they attend. The laboratory method, when successful, tends to train the participant's focus on how he can learn on "real time" as he plays his various roles in the system.

Finally, the laboratory method is more congruent than the didactic one with the process conception of consultation. One feature of a well-run laboratory is that if it runs off course it can correct itself through the actions of participants and staff. The corrective processes are, in fact, the meat of the experience. The more didactic approach of planned seminars often does quite well at providing information, but it does not have this self-correcting, process-oriented quality. The structure of more traditional teaching sessions is often such that they break down when participants attempt to influence the process. This is bad training for both participants and staff. The more controlling and uninfluenceable a program is, the less effective it is as a training ground for consultants and clients. It takes their focus away from influencing process and turns it toward the more traditional, static definition of consultation as an object to be provided by a salesman.

6. The Compleat Consultant's Costume Catalogue

To this point, I have presented a fairly single-minded emphasis on learning, growth, role confirmation, competence, development, and the like. It may all sound a bit loaded, with too much goodness and not enough truth so far as the real difficulties in helping others are concerned.

This mood reflects another major dilemma in learning to help: we want to see "the Way" and work so hard at staring that we do not see that much of what is actually happening. The business of helping others is so ephemeral and so dependent for success on the process used (not just good techniques and better intentions) that it is hard to perceive clearly.

Sometimes the way to see clearly is not to bang away head-on at "important" ideas or problems, but rather to come at them from another angle, in a spirit of play rather than work, and just see what happens. I believe that consultants do too little of this and therefore make it difficult for themselves to see new patterns and to give up old ones.[1]

In this chapter I should like to demonstrate what I mean by a looser process and at the same time give myself and the reader a slight breather from the heavy concepts at hand. The subject is the nonverbal symbolic sartorial communication of consultant to client, roughly translated as creative costuming for fun and profit.

Although written in the eminently practical form of a catalogue (inspired by Mr. L. L. Bean), there are also some

1. Being paid by the hour or the day may induce a slight tinge of guilt in the consultant who tries to loosen up and play with his process.

theoretical issues strewn throughout for those who care to look for them. The issues concern symbolic identification, the establishment and maintenance of power differentials, interpersonal perception of similarities and differences and their effects on credibility, the impact of consultant image on client motivations, and several more mystical points which will be obvious to the average (and better than average) reader.

As you read this chapter, you may experience some problems with your own reactions to it. You may see it as a mistake, a chapter from another book that was accidentally sandwiched in here by the publisher. Or, you may see it as intentionally placed here, but only through very poor judgment. You may even feel that whoever did it ought to be horsewhipped.

If any of these describe your reactions, you belong to a fairly large group, including a number of reviewers and pre-publication readers. Several people urged me not to include this chapter, and labels for it ranged from "interesting" through "irrelevant" to "malevolent."

After considerable soul-searching, I realized that the difficulty in making a decision represented exactly why I should include this chapter in this book. One of the points I tried to illustrate with it was that consultants tend to throw away (or fail to recognize) some of their best data: those feelings, intuitions, fantasies, and the like that are seen as irrelevant interruptions or failures of professionalism. As I noted a moment ago, a number of useful dimensions of the consultant-client relationship are illustrated through the costume catalogue; but since they became visible when I was playing with my fantasies rather than "working" on a diagnosis, I have been very susceptible to arguments that they have no place in a "serious" book. To the contrary. I think that they are the tip of an iceberg of intuitions and insights about my own work with clients. I only wish that I knew how to hoist the whole thing out of the water.

Style and Consulting

In the ebb and flow of process between helper and client, *the style* with which one does something is at least as important as the *content* of what he does. In most cases it is more important, since the style can be traced back to the performer, while the content is often interred with the bones of never-to-be-read diagnostic reports.

I should not say that style has been totally overlooked as a consulting variable, only that theoreticians have been very selective in those aspects of style which they have analyzed. They have tended I believe, to be overly concerned with certain rather obvious aspects of the consultant's role, such as how much actual help he provides to the client, how effective he is at training the client to help himself, and how aggressive he is in his encounters with the client. I will admit that these have some relevance to whether anything of any note results from a consultation, although I am safe in saying that this has never been actually proved.[2] However, the importance of these aspects of style fades to a shadow compared with a factor which to my knowledge has been totally neglected by every behavioral scientist who has to date studied the helping process: the *style of clothing* worn by the consultant, and the manner in which he wears his clothes.

Elsewhere I have put forward the thesis that most encounters between client and consultant are massive examples of double presentation-of-self exercises being carried out under the handicap of having to pretend that some sort of task is being done at the same time.

The important measure of success, given this view, is not whether an interpersonal event led to change, or to greater understanding, but rather whether it led to the client seeing the

2. I feel safe in this assertion, because it came to me in a flash of insight one day (I think) that in the behavioral sciences, nothing had ever been proved (and even this has not been proved). The best that we can say with certainty from the most elaborate of research designs is that somebody cared enough about some question to design and carry out that elaborate research design (assuming, of course, that we believe them . . . which I usually do).

consultant in the manner in which the consultant wanted to be seen. Not to be overly technical, it could be expressed by the following equation: $(I_a = I_d (.25 I_p + .15 V + .60 CL) + Y)$, where I_a is the actual image of the consultant in client's eyes; I_d is the image which the consultant desires to create; I_p is the previous image, which the client carries into the present encounter with the consultant; V is the verbal propaganda which the consultant spews out; CL is the impact of the clothes the consultant is wearing; and Y is a general correction factor, roughly standing for "You never can tell for sure."

This equation was arrived at through much detailed data collection and analysis. The weights are those which best predicted the description of the consultant that a client would provide when asked for a description of a consultant out of context by someone not in his family, his advertising agency, or their affiliates.[3]

From the equation, it becomes immediately obvious which factor is the important one if you want to systematically increase a consultant's ability to manage his image in the eyes of the client. Unfortunately, that factor is Y, about which we still know nothing to speak of. I and my colleagues at the institute therefore decided to settle for the next-best strategy, which was to develop the constructive use of clothing (CL) as a path to influencing style in consulting.

Whatever the difficulties in our early methods of selecting the crucial variable for study, once we chose it we got cracking. We enlisted the aid of over twenty qualified and unqualified consultants who went forth into the field to experiment with different styles of dress in order to see what the effect would be on their client systems. We waited until consultants had insinuated themselves into various client systems and then had our consultants alter their styles of dress wherever they could find a handy spot to change. This entailed some risks, not the least of which were overexposure and/or arrest for same. Exposure, as we well knew, is something that a consultant must watch very carefully. It is easy to wear out one's welcome with a client, particularly if one is surprised

3. The reader will appreciate, I am sure, the difficulties we had in finding interviewers who fulfilled all three of these criteria.

in nothing but his shorts and shoes. The damage to a relationship is often irreparable in such an instance, particularly if one is wearing the wrong kind of shoes. Shorts, on the other hand, make almost no difference. There are a great number of degrees of freedom in shorts.

At any rate, I am happy to report that all the technical difficulties were eventually resolved, and the study was completed. The remainder of this chapter is one of the fruits of this research: a catalogue of the line of products which the institute is now able to offer to consultants who have become aware of the extent to which their relationship with their client is affected by the clothes they wear. The items listed here are by no means the only ones available. The interested reader can send his name and address to us and receive by return mail our complete catalogue in a plain brown wrapper.[4]

This catalogue is in itself somewhat of a consultant's aid, since it sharpens those aspects of the consultant-client relationship which are most amenable to influence through the presentation-of-self medium. It should also be noted that not all of the items listed below can be worn by all consultants. Those which are selective are marked with an asterisk. We will not specifically list those who cannot effectively use them, since you should already know who you are.

The reader will probably notice that some of our items are illustrated, while others are only described. This, we are sad to report, is due to our relatively low level of trust in our readers. Competent you may well be; Honest? We are not so sure. Therefore we do not show those items which could be acquired only from us or by copying from this report. Perhaps some day this precaution will not be necessary. We certainly hope so. But for now we have to be content with weaving a fabric of words to help you see the possibilities inherent in proper consultant costuming.

J–294. This is a New York Yankees baseball uniform, complete with cap, fielder's glove, and spikes. It features your name written across the back and an award patch on

4. Or, since plain brown wrappers are more difficult to find these days than is our catalogue, we will alternately send you a plain brown wrapper mailed inside the catalogue.

the left shoulder, with the name of the award sewn in with thread in illegible longhand script. This outfit was specially designed to be donned during those crucial periods of a project when the client is questioning whether or not you are really a member of the team. Nothing direct need be said. When you show up for a meeting in this smart number, the implication will be planted in his mind subliminally. He may not know quite why, but he will see you in a different and more favorable light. It might be of interest to note that when we developed this model, we originally used a Cincinnati Reds uniform, with mixed results. It tended to sow the seeds of ideological differences, particularly with clients in business, so it was abandoned for the Yankee uniform. *A warning note:* those consultants working with Southern white citizens' organizations in the United States would be well advised to develop alternative means of demonstrating their team spirit, such as using a bleached-out version of item D-1408 shown later.

J–297. This is a loosely fitting blue suit covered completely with first-quality mirrors, all two inches square. When working well, it provides an integrated reflection which makes it appear that you are wearing exactly what the client is wearing.[5] This outfit was designed mainly for that important initial contact with the client where he is anxious about whether or not you are "his kind of person," and where you are anxious to show him that you are. When the suit is working well, and all the mirrors are aligned correctly, the two of you will look like the Bobbsey Twins to him (although not to an outside observer). Unfortunately, when they are not projecting a smooth image, there is a slight tendency to look as though you are wearing a baggy, sequined cape. This has been known to put certain clients off a bit, especially if they have emotional problems in the masculinity-femininity area. In its favor, it should also be said that this outfit is the only one of our line that can be used with almost any type of client, since it takes its visual content from the client himself. It is particularly useful for work with a group of clients,

5. For best results, client and consultant should be of approximately the same sex.

where you can project a different (and acceptable) image to each without any actual change in behavior on your own part.

J–303. Our "I'm just one of the boys" line, in two versions, as shown in figure 4. This is a particularly useful costume for work with client systems which see themselves as part of the Now Generation, although it is of little use to consultants who identify themselves with either the Then Group or the Later Movement. The basic components are some kind of uniform jacket, guaranteed to be of not later than 1954 vintage, baggy khaki or corduroy pants, a cap (two models to choose from), loafers, and beard (again two choices). The brick wall shown in the illustration is optional but can be purchased at a discount if acquired with the rest of the outfit. It is very useful for establishing dominance (fig. 4, A) or setting limits (fig. 4, B) on the contractual relationship.

J–304. The "I'm not just one of the boys" model, which is shown in figure 5. This number is to be used particularly for establishing a certain social distance between yourself and your clients. It is also useful for developing in oneself a sense of the terrible social importance of one's job and the dangers bordering the path to doing it. The outfit comes complete with pipe and seven collars, three of which have been pre-soiled to provide that special touch of struggle and sacrifice which really sets the tone for those situations in which this model is appropriate. We should note that this has been one of our most popular items, although we cannot say exactly why this should be. It is possible that the use of this model has a tendency to drive out competitive models, so that when one consultant uses it, his colleagues are also forced to use it in order to regain visibility with the client. *A note of warning:* under no circumstances should this model be worn while consulting with a religious organization. It will be considered passé and/or an attempt to communicate the J–303 message of "I'm just one of the boys." The J–304 is a very sensitive instrument, and it must be tuned to the type of system with which it is used.

*D-211.** Our Super-Tek model. This number is definitely

FIG. 4. J–303, Versions *A* and *B* of "I'm Just One of the Boys"

FIG. 5. J–304, "I'm Not Just One of the Boys"

not for everyone. Those who are claustrophobic would be well advised to consider it beyond their range. For others, however, this outfit could be an absolute must. It was designed for consulting work with technically oriented organizations such as research and development firms. Historically, these have been notably difficult for the consultant who is trying to establish credibility with scientific types. As you can see in figure 6, this model is no half-way job. Without coming right out and saying it, it leaves the client with a very strong impression that you've "been there too," possibly even more so than the client himself. There are several notes to be added for this model. One is that the instructions on the suit itself should *not* (repeat, not) be followed as to inside pressure. If used in this manner in the average meeting room, the suit has a definite propensity to explode, which can be disruptive to whatever point you happen to be making at the time. Use our handy pressure guide ($12 extra) instead. A second is that the cost of this model is significantly higher (roughly $140,200) than any other one in our line. Perhaps one day this will not be so, but for the present it can be considered simply one of the prices which must be paid for *true* innovation. Third, mobility is definitely restricted in this suit. If at any time while using it you are required to gesture, such as while making a point at a newsprint chart, be sure to raise the *left* arm, which has the indicator band around it (see arrow in fig. 6). Under these conditions, avoid raising the right arm unless absolutely necessary, since this motion activates the waste system in the suit. Finally, when ordering this model, please include with your check a signed statement addressed to us telling us that you do not know where you got the suit. This is a simple precaution which we must take because of patent difficulties that are still being worked out.

D-33a. This is a real specialty of our program, a fully-anodized suit of armor, complete with shield, battle-ax, and two visors so that the inside coating of one may be cleaned while the other is being used. This suit was designed particularly for that special occasion when you are giving negative criticism to an aggressive client or colleague. This armor can

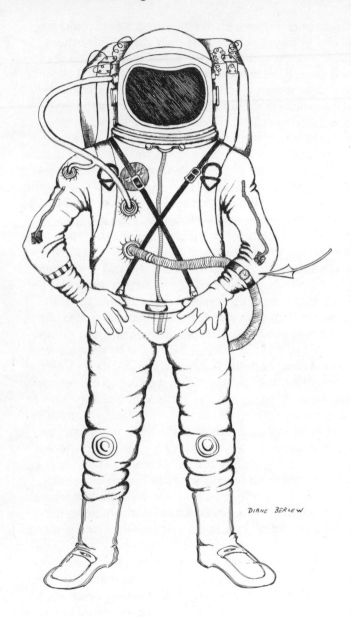

FIG. 6. D–211, Super-Tek

literally make you impervious to any unruly flare-ups which might mistakenly occur as you help the receiver toward becoming a better person.[6] A special feature of this suit of armor is its double flexing greve joints on both arms and legs. This means that you can step into it backwards and have the same mobility as if you were facing frontwards (which is, to be honest, less than 100 percent). This is an excellent strategy when you are engaged in third party confrontation tactics and expect that there will be attacks from the rear. A special peephole in the back of the helmet allows you to appear to be facing north while being able to be actually looking south. *A word of warning:* while in the reverse position, it is unfortunate but true that if there is a more direct client who attacks you head-on, face-to-face (he thinks), he will have a field day.

L–943.* While many of the above numbers, such as the suit of armor, are intended to be worn by consultants of either (or any) sex, we have one particular combination package which is designed especially for the female side (fig. 7, *A* and *B*). Model *A,* Authority Speaks, is for those women who wish to emphasize the authoritative aspect of their role vis à vis the client, particularly when there are power issues within the client system. This outfit tends to quickly crystallize those issues and bring matters to a head.[7] Our staff reports that this is a particularly effective strategy with civilian defense contractors, who can never be totally certain, if you are wearing a uniform, that you are not a member of their board of directors. This costume, on the other hand, is not recommended for consultation work in a university setting, unless your goal is the rapid polarization of issues.

Model *B,* on the other hand, is our Show-Business Gala, specially designed for work with those clients who want an aura of glamour from their consultant. Our experience has been that many clients feel that they are more than getting their money's worth if their consultant is involved somehow with the public, as an author, talk-show guest, or what have

6. This is very useful in keeping the phrase "This hurts me more than it does you" in the realm of euphemism.
7. Or was it to a boil? Or boil to a head? No matter, I suppose.

FIG. 7. L–943, *A*, Authority Speaks; *B*, Show-Business Gala

you. With model *B* and our two-week course in basic great
theatrical gestures, you will provide the client with his taste
of glamour without having to actually say that you have ever
performed in anything. *A gentle reminder:* it is not recommended that the wearer of this model engage in strenuous
nonverbal exercises with the client, unless she is prepared for
a certain amount of unpredictable variation in her costume.
Working lunches of Italian food must also be discouraged.

We should also inform the reader that there is a version of
model *A*, Authority Speaks, for the male consultant as well.
It is M–943, as shown in figure 8. No more will be said
about it here, since it speaks for itself.

D-777. This is our Two-by-Two special, consisting of two
integral parts as shown in figure 9. Part *A* is a pair of short
pants and a sweatshirt, designed to project an air of naive
helplessness. This has been found to be useful in reducing
the most difficult obstacle in the consultant's role: the client's tendency to see the consultant as powerful, overbearing,
and superior. The short pants are guaranteed to nullify these
feelings, and even reverse them. The client's fear of the consultant will be reduced to a mere fraction of its former level,
especially if part *A* is accompanied by a line of chatter about
the weather, latest football results, and finding some broads.

But part *A* is totally incomplete without part *B,* also
shown in figure 9. No consultant really wants to be looked
upon as less powerful than his client, thus the use of *B* after
an initial contact wearing *A*. After lulling the client into
an off-guard stance, the consultant arrives wearing a very
smartly tailored suit with a trim hat, gloves, and an umbrella
which is conspicuously equipped with a sword.[8] This array
impresses the client with the consultant's overwhelming
power and sophistication, as well as reduces the client's overbearing air of superiority which was transferred from you to
him through the use of part *A*. *No shortcuts:* note once again
that this is a complete set and is not to be used in separate
pieces. Our research has shown that the most helpful relationship is one which does not stabilize at either position,

8. The umbrella comes equipped with an easy-to-operate catch for
"accidental" releases of the sword at the proper moments.

FIG. 8. M–943, Authority Speaks (Male Version)

FIG. 9. D–777, Special Set, The Two-by-Two

DIANE BERLEW

that is, with the consultant one-up or with the client one-up.
Maximum growth, in both competence and fees, has been
found to rest with wide swings between these two poles.

D–1408. This is another combination piece, called our
Inscrutable East model. The two versions are shown in figure
10, parts *A* and *B*. They are not so closely tied to one another as the Two-by-Two, but using them together does
enhance the power of each. Part *A* is designed for the consultant who wishes to send the message to the client that he
(the consultant) comes from a culture where the norms and
values are so different that there is no telling what he might
do in the present situation.[9] This we refer to technically as
predictability inscrutability (pi). By his clothing the consultant establishes that he could and might do almost anything at any given time, and the client will not be able to
receive cues from him as to when he will do it. A subtle but
consistent wild caste to the eye helps considerably in creating
this mood.

Part *B*, by contrast, is designed to give the client as little
data as possible, about the consultant or anything else. Its
main feature is a large wraparound sheet and a pair of clog
shoes (see again fig. 10, part *B*), so that no feature of the
consultant can actually be seen by the client. This is technically known as *visibility inscrutability* (vi). The client does
not know whether to expect you to be unpredictable or not;
in fact, in field testing this model we had several instances
where the client forgot that the consultant was there at all.
This was moderately useful for unobtrusive observation of
behavior but proved to be notably unsuccessful when the
consultant was attempting to intervene. In the worst instance, he was accidentally locked into the client's office
building for the night. In both of these versions, the goal is
to infuse the relationship with that air of mystery and mys-
tique that can be so handy at certain key moments in a
consultation, such as when a client resists what you are suggesting. There is nothing like (pi) or (vi) to make him think
twice about upsetting you. *Please pay attention:* this particu-

9. Unless, of course, one is consulting with a firm of belligerent
warriors.

lar set loses its effectiveness faster than any other. Repeated wearings of these costumes will reduce their inscrutability markedly. Our data indicate that five wearings render them semiscrutable in the eyes of the client, while with more than ten applications you are as open to scrutiny as if you were not wearing them at all.

M–400.* This number is not, strictly speaking, a whole outfit. It is only a jacket, but what a jacket!! It is called our Monzo the Magnificent Magician's Mantle and is shown in figure 11. This jacket was designed for that one consultant in four who aspires to a higher standard and wishes to continually amaze and confound the client with his feats of wizardry. The predominant feature of the jacket is the size and placement of its pockets. As you can see in the illustration, they are both huge and mostly hidden. This allows the consultant great flexibility in how and when he presents things to the client. Reports, papers, quips, and the like can be made to appear as if plucked out of thin air. Need we say that this is also a great one for wearing around the house, or out in crowds at the race track?[10] The special cloth cap worn in the illustration is not included in M–400 but can be ordered concurrently. It is unusually roomy and can accommodate rapid changes in head size. This also makes it a fine companion piece to the Two-by-Two set already described. *Sorry to say:* the polka dot tie shown was one of a kind made expressly for Monzo and is not for sale.

B–747. And, finally, we come to the latest (but we hope not the last) in our current line, the fabulous Quick Attention-Getter model, with which we have had gratifying success after gratifying success. Here are the features which are shown in figure 12:[11] a rough leather tunic which suggests to the client that you are connected in very elemental ways to the whole collective unconscious of the human race and that of other races as well, a huge leather belt with a

10. The advantages of this jacket in relation to the pickpocketing process are two: tremendous storage space if you are the pickpocket, and a never-ending labyrinth of confusing passages if you are the pickpocket's quarry.

11. Modeled, incidentally, by the senior author himself (fig. 12).

FIG. 10. D–1408, Our Inscrutable East Models

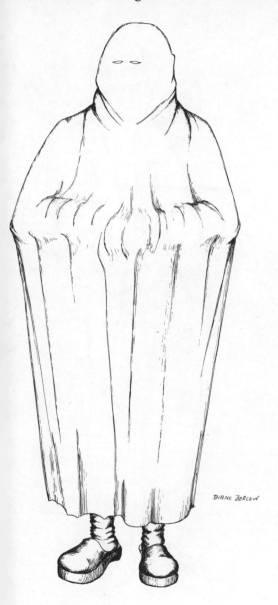

FIG. 11. M–400, Monzo the Magnificent Magician's Mantle

FIG. 12. B–747, The Quick Attention-Getter

giant square silver buckle which shows that you are as up-to-date in fashion as any Madison Avenue ad man, a set of leather slippers and ankle thongs which will endear you to any underground client group (in a slightly cheaper version you receive a brown magic marker with which to paint on the thongs), and a genuine goatskin jacket with an authentic rip from armpit to wrist for easy arm wrestling (the goatskin comes with a six-month supply of goat aroma spray so that you will never be caught half-safe: you can constantly be demonstrating to the client that you are liberated from straight society.[12] *Bad luck, but it could be worse:* the boulder is not included in the package. However, for so long as they last, we do have a limited supply of boulders guaranteed to be not less than thirty-two inches in diameter. These can be purchased for a nominal sum from our recently established quarry division.

These are the items which are currently available. All of them are based on our painstaking research and are guaranteed to change your routine, dull, consulting life in marked ways. We intend to continue our developments and to expand the line to include aspects such as Menus for Entertaining Clients, Background Music for Every Consulting Encounter, and so on. We are confident that our pioneering work stands alone in the annals of consulting theory and research, as well as in the commercial exploitation thereof.

In closing I can add only that we are all too well aware of the old adage Clothes Do not Make the Man. Nor can we find any very satisfactory reply to this. But our efforts are only slightly dimmed by this unkind cut, for we have literally hundreds of interesting letters from customers who have tried our line. However, since space is short, and so is the budget alloted for publication, those testimonials will have to wait until another day. I will say only that it was most gratifying to hear from Henry Kissinger so soon after he tried the Quick Attention Getter at the White House.

12. For a very slight extra charge, we will provide a can of spray which deadens your sense of smell and liberates you from the effects of your goatskin.

7. Teamwork in Consultation

In this chapter I will examine the dynamics of the collaborative process between consultants who are working together as a team on a planned change project.[1] I see the quality of consultants' relationships with one another as a particularly important influence on the consulting process. The greater the demand for systematic change and organizational development efforts, the more likely it is that resources and skills will be required in any given project which are far beyond the range and energies of a single person. Effective consultation in the future will demand that consultants work together, and this in turn creates a necessity that they be effective in dealing with one another as well as with the client.

It does not take a great deal of subtlety to realize that how a consultant team collaborates will have an impact on what kinds of change they are able to effect in a client system. This follows from the well-accepted observation that interpersonal processes influence how effectively a group of people are able to work on a task. As Bennis et al. (1973) summarize, we know that the nature of a relationship influences its productivity, its likelihood of being satisfying to the parties involved, and the innovative quality of what is produced.

In spite of this awareness, however, there has been very little attention paid to interaction among consultants in literature on the consultative process. Even though behavioral

1. For the sake of convenience, *team* will mean simply two or more consultants who are jointly responsible for a planned change project with a client system or group.

scientists know that the quality of interaction influences task relationships, this view has not been applied very often to the *consultants'* interaction with each other. Research reports tend to provide data almost exclusively about the consultant-client relationship, or about events between clients. For example, here is an excerpt from a critique I wrote of a case study in behavioral science intervention.

> Like most other cases written about planned change, it was much clearer in narrating events in the clients' world than in highlighting relevant events in the consultants' world or in the joint world inhabited by both. . . . the issue of conflicts *within* the consulting group over appropriate strategies was raised early, whetted my appetite, and then faded away. One paragraph tells us that "within CMHC itself there was considerable tension during the initial weeks of the dispute, as conflicting pressures were placed on the CMHC staff . . ." while the next paragraph says: "After some preliminary planning was completed, CMHC approached Local Group leaders and invited them to collaborate in sponsoring and implementing an open meeting aimed at managing conflict." Whoops! What happened to the tension and disagreement within the CMHC staff? How did CMHC members get themselves together enough to pick this course of action? For me this is an example of a general problem in reports on change: the process of collaboration within the consultant team has received little description and less analysis. [1970, pp. 361–62]

This chapter is designed to be a kind of map to help bridge this gap. I consider this a worthwhile topic, because I believe that the consultant-consultant relationship has some special dynamics to it which are related to its nature and structure. The fact that the relationship is formed to try to effect change means that it will tend to be under more stress than one formed for a routine task performance. The fact that the task is consultation means that there is always a third party implicitly involved: the client or client system. No matter where the consultants are physically located, the client is also there by implication. This complicates the process of interaction between consultants as do other attributes of the role which will be discussed shortly.

Reasons for Collaboration

Before going further with the aspects of consultant collaboration that are special and create special problems, I think it would be useful to look for a moment at why consultants work together in the first place. Why do they combine their efforts, and what kinds of functions does collaboration fulfill for them? If we have a clearer picture of how people get together, we are better able to describe the kinds of problems they are likely to experience.

The most obvious reason for collaboration among consultants is that a limited volume of work can be done singly, and the number of places in which one person can be at once is also limited. Having another person involved in a project often means that observation, data collection, or intervention can take place on two different fronts at the same time. A second reason why collaboration takes place is just as important: it is the instance where each one who is party to the relationship has some particular area of specialization which he can contribute to the consulting or T-group work so that the members form a complementary unit. The resources which each person brings to the task may be recognized in advance or may be discovered only through actual collaboration itself; and often new skills or abilities are developed through this process. The specializations may be in different aspects of the behavioral side of consultation, or they may be in very different basic disciplines, as when a social psychologist and a computer sciences expert join together to effect change in a client's information systems. This latter case of different disciplines will be discussed more specifically near the end of this chapter.

A third reason for collaboration is that working together in a joint staff relationship provides a way out of the kind of isolation which people are prone to experience when they are doing change work. A change agent often is not a member of the system which he is trying to change, whether this be a T-group or a functioning task group in an organization. To the extent that the change agent is seen as someone trying to horn in, or influence a situation unjustly, he tends to be pushed out or isolated from the ongoing group. Given this separateness, the presence of another consultant can be a very significant asset in dealing with feelings of isolation and in providing a sense of connectedness which one could not ordinarily get from the system with which he is operating. An important aspect of this connectedness is the satisfaction which comes from simply having another professional at hand who is able to speak the same language as yourself. This is an essential process when difficult problems are being faced, and there is no one in the client system who either particularly cares to or is able to discuss their problem in the kind of depth which you are used to exploring as a professional.[2]

I suspect that another function of collaboration is a need to extend responsibility for intervention to two or more people instead of leaving it all on one person's shoulders. I do not know how often this would be admitted as a reason for collaboration, or how conscious it is, but I am sure that it does play some part in the process. Yet another aspect of shared responsibility is that having another person as a team member means that you are not totally dependent on yourself for diagnostic insights or design of action interventions. With joint responsibility, there tends to be less anxiety on each person's part about whether he alone will come up with whatever appropriate thing will move a client group forward at a given time.

One more function which working with someone else on a change project serves is that of just getting to know him better. The consulting situation, where continuing insights into process and the ability to create new action intervention are very valuable skills, provides people in a team relationship with quite a bit of information about one another. There

2. For a broader discussion of the demands of the consulting role, see chapter eight, "Consultants and Detectives."

are many stressful situations where there are opportunities to see the other person in different behavioral modes, especially comparing his responses to stress with that of yourself and your clients.

In live consulting, there is also a normative system in which behavior of each person is much more under scrutiny than in the average collaborative process. This self-examination can lead to each person getting to know one another better than would often be true in a much longer relationship in another context. In a sense, the consultants *have* to get to know one another well and be able to connect with one another in order to be of much help to the client system. I should also reemphasize the shared stress aspect of the consulting process: after a difficult client contact or an involved T-group laboratory, I have often felt much closer to a colleague because of our shared experience, in the same way that two people feel closer when they have worked side by side sandbagging a dike during a flood. Not only is this acquaintance process an outcome of consulting together, it has been (in my own and others' choices of partners) a reason for taking on a project and calling a certain group of people together to work on it.

To summarize briefly, these are some of the reasons why joint consultation takes place: there is too much to do alone; different skills or training are often needed; joint consultation provides someone to talk to, to share responsibility with, and to get to know better. Next I will discuss some of the forces which operate on that collaborative relationship once it has been formed.

Forces on a Consulting Team

We can divide the forces which operate on a consulting team into three very rough categories: those forces whose main source is *inside* the team, those whose source is *outside* the team (from other people), and those forces whose existence is attributable to the *nature of the task* which is being performed. These are not meant to be totally discrete categories, nor are they a scale in any sense; they simply summarize the main sources of pressure which consultants have described to me and which I myself have felt in the consulting role.

Forces Inside the Team

Forces inside the team are of several kinds. One is the set of feelings which the consultants have about one another and their communication of those feelings. These feelings can help or hinder a good consultation process, depending on the needs of the consultants, the particular situation, and the means through which they are handled. A related force is the set of expectations which each consultant has about himself and the other members in terms of professional behavior and competence. In a sense, these expectations come from outside the team, i.e., they have their source in the profession in general, but they are transmitted most powerfully by the team members themselves. Another force or factor is the way in which the team is organized: the structures they have built for decision making, allocating work and roles, and so on. Finally, the personal styles of the team members influence its process: the values, assumptions about means, past training, and intrapersonal and interpersonal needs of each member play a part in influencing the other members and the team as a whole. The kinds of situations with which each consultant is comfortable help determine what kind of resource he will be and what kind of influence he will have on the other team members.

Forces from Outside the Team

Forces from outside the team are generally attempts of one sort or another to influence individuals on the team or the team as a whole. The client system is a major source of this type of influence. The reactions, responses, and initiations of a client all provide data about the nature of his expectations of how the consultants perform their roles. The client system influences the team not only with messages about expectations, but also through the choices the system makes as to where to put its energies and resources. For example, those things which are crucial to a change project (such as planning) must be done by someone, and when clients hold back on them the team often must step in to fill the gap. Looking at group process during a task session is a common example of an area where the client can often seduce the consultants into doing what should ultimately be the client's work.

Another source of outside influence is the profession of consulting in general. As I noted, this is usually carried in through the internalized values of the team members themselves; but there are also more direct forces, as when a question of ethics or professional competence arises, and some outside agency becomes involved.

The third major outside influence is the network of other people with whom the team members are involved. Most consultants are involved in a variety of roles, some professional and some personal. All of these roles compete for the time and energy of a consulting team member, and this competition often creates internal conflicts in the team and reduces contacts between members. Consultants, in my experience, tend to overcommit themselves and to be unrealistic about how much they can do. This stretching can be disguised a bit when one is consulting alone, but it becomes much more obvious when he is a part of a team which has made commitments. When he falls behind, it may influence the sequence of steps for the whole team.

The Nature of the Task

The nature of the task refers to the rather specific qualities of the task of changing social systems. These qualities themselves have an influence on the process of a consulting team. For instance, when the basic task is change in behavior or structure, people in the client system are likely to have strong feelings about the process, much more likely than if the task were some routine operation. People develop vested interests, rationalized explanations for why certain choices were made, and other world-views which are tied up with their sense of self-competence. When these world-views are called into question, no matter how gently, feelings of conflict, threat, and/or embarrassment tend to be aroused. These feelings make the consultant role one which carries more stress and potential guilt ("Look what I am doing to those people") than many other roles, and this stress must be dealt with by the team.

Another aspect of the task is its ambiguity: the absence of many rules about what is right and wrong, what needs to be done, and who ought to be doing it. Success is partly determined by how it is measured, and in consulting the measures are relatively fuzzy as compared, for instance, with accounting. Perception of success of an intervention often depends as much on the perceiver's filters as it does on the effect on the client system. This tends to lead toward internal conflicts within a team over both means and ends, even though the common goal of more healthy social systems and more healthy individuals is paid verbal homage.

Finally, the ambiguity is exacerbated by the long time scales which are often required in order to determine whether or not a consultation has been effective. Emotional conflicts within a team could sometimes be resolved through relevant feedback from the client system, but in many instances the data will unfortunately not be available until long after the conflict has been either resolved or swept under the rug. In fact, conflicts often occur within a team over the issue of time scale itself, since very often it is not clear what the time parameters of a particular change problem really are.

These, then, are some of the forces which act upon a team engaged in a consulting project. Summarized they include expectations about performance of roles, stresses due to the very human nature of the task, and the effects of the ambiguity of the task. Each of these forces can work for positive or negative results, depending on how they are handled. Expectations from inside and outside the team can provide a stimulus for achievement and self-examination; they can also produce tremendous role conflicts when there is a difference of expectations between the consultants and clients, the consultants on the team, or within a single consultant as he tries to sort out his own conflicting priorities. The emotional side to the process of change is an enlivening force which creates a feeling of involvement that more mechanical tasks could never create; it also increases the emotional stresses on the consultants and makes the job more psychologically demanding than many others. The ambiguity allows room for experimentation and innovation if the consultants' sense of personal security is high. If it is not, the ambiguity of the task can be a continual drain on the energy of the team.

Whether the positive or negative effects will occur, and in what proportion, is a function of the strength of the forces, such as the fervor with which a client group demands that the consultants be the way they (the clients) think a consultant should be. In the next section I will describe the most likely "pathologies" which occur when the forces on the team balance out in the negative direction.

Pathologies in Team Consultation

The following list of symptoms illustrates the kind of negative effects which are likely to arise from team consultation. They are by no means the only problems which can arise in this process, but they do represent some of the most potent sources of consultant team ineffectiveness. They have been compiled from three sources: my own experience as a member of various consulting teams; interviews about and tapes of collaborative consultation projects; and my and others' experiences as cotrainers in laboratory training groups, where the dynamics of the relationship of consultants to group (and to each other) are, as I have argued earlier, often prototypic of other team-client relationships yet are more sharply focused and therefore more open to analysis by the group and the consultants.

Discontinuity

When more than one consultant is working on a change project, the potential for discontinuity is higher than if there is just one consultant. By discontinuity, I mean a lack of connection between the action steps and interventions made by the consultants over a period of time. This occurs when processes that are set in motion are not allowed to be worked through to some kind of conclusion. They are short-circuited by the same or different member of the consulting team who has something new that *he* wants to try, something that runs in a different direction from the previous process. As an example, here, from my notes, is one consultant's comment on this problem within his group.

> One of the things that is difficult for me is the way that steps are not carried through. We have a tendency to make a diagnosis, work with the client on an initial action plan, and then abandon the plan when it's about one-third along. Ray is particularly likely to push for dropping the old plan, no matter what it is. We don't work enough with the client on how plans will change and what this means for them.[3]

This quote suggests that discontinuity is intimately tied to the issue of flexibility. The opposite of discontinuity is not a stiff, unthinking follow-through regardless of changed circumstances; but rather a flexible design for action which has processes for checks and changes built into it, so that the client can experience the thrust of the change process as having a wholeness to it. Although consultants may be able to function reasonably well with what looks to the client as somewhat random changes in direction, to the client these changes will feel unrelated and discontinuous with respect to a long-term change strategy.

Forces toward discontinuity come mainly from within a consulting team, often because of unresolved differences over the basic goals or methods of a particular change project.

3. Wherever names are used, they are fictitious ones which bear no relationship to those originally mentioned.

The different styles of the various consultants get acted out in this manner, with each step making sense for itself but not particularly connected with those before or after it. Ambiguity also contributes somewhat to this process, as do the reinforcements of clients who are more oriented toward short-term experiences for their own sake.

Vectorization

Vectorization is a concept which is related to discontinuity, in that the consultants on a team are working at cross purposes and creating forces or "vectors" influencing the client system in conflicting directions.[4] Vectorization differs from discontinuity in that the vectors problem occurs simultaneously, at a particular point in time, while the discontinuity pattern is seen over a series of events that do not relate to each other.

Perhaps a better term for vectors would be *resultants,* because the question is, what is the resultant of the forces that two or more consultants are applying to a client system? Do the forces work in the same direction, intensifying the experience, or do they tend to work in opposite directions and cancel one another out?

An example of conflicting vectors is the T-group situation where one trainer is attempting to help people to express their feelings of anxiety and sometimes deep sorrow, while the other trainer is attempting to work on a group process level and to get them to talk about what they are learning about the way groups evolve. The resultant of these two forces often will be a kind of flickering or wavering back and forth between discussion of feelings and intellectualization, without very much movement taking place in either direction.

4. I owe this notion mainly to my work with Barry Oshry. We discovered the vector notion while cotraining in a T-group. It was first named while playing Ping-Pong, when we noticed that the resultant of conflicting ideas about what shot to make was generally the sum of the two vectors causing the conflict. The resultant usually did not amount to much of a shot.

This flickering effect is not the only outcome of the consultants' differences. It is possible to establish a working pattern where they work in series with one another, bringing complementary skills to a total group process. If they fall into operating in a win-lose competition, however, they will tend to be applying their different directions at the same time and therefore will be pulling the group in a manner which results in not much useful movement in either direction.

As implied above, the main force for vectorization tends to come from inside the team, especially from issues around competition, style differences, and differing interpersonal needs. These internal forces are often amplified by client responses, as will be discussed below.

Contagion

By contagion I mean literally the process whereby one person or group picks up or takes on the virus, sickness, or "bug" of another person or group. In the present context, this refers specifically to the tendency of consultant and client groups who are interacting to pass on their problems, symptoms, and styles to one another.

This transfer process works as a two-way street. In one direction, the consultant team often begins to show signs of the conflicts, styles, and emotional stresses which typify the client system. Here are one consultant's observations on this.

> You know how it goes—the longer you're around someone, the more you pick up things from them. You might not even know it, but it's happening just the same. We did a job for a company where secrecy was the most important thing to them. Everything had to be hidden unless somebody could produce a strong reason why it shouldn't be. In our work with them we got more and more guarded. Mostly with them, but even a bit with ourselves. It wasn't planned, it was just that secrecy was more on our minds.

Later he added that in planning sessions the consultants spoke openly about their lack of love for the system's closedness, yet they still became a bit more like them. In a similar manner, emotional flareups in a client group have been observed to come just before similar emotionality occurs in a consulting team. The themes were similar enough to indicate that the clients' behavior had touched off feelings, associations, and fantasies in the consultants which made these same issues more likely to come out among the consultant team. Cotrainers in a T-group report a similar pattern to the ebb and flow of issues between themselves.

In the other direction, the client system also picks up the issues and pathologies of the consulting team. An extreme but illuminating example of this is the research of Gladstone and Burkham, who found a connection in a mental hospital between hidden staff disagreements and the incidence of pathological symptoms in patients (1966). Along this line, anxiety feelings are probably the most contagious commodity which can be passed from consultant to client system.

Both these forms of contagion mean that the consulting team must be aware of process issues in each group and be willing to deal with them openly (especially since the research just cited offers some proof that they cannot be ignored and thereby have no effect). Contagion tends to have a mixed effect, though. On the negative side, it makes the client and consultant groups look different from their normal state. On the other hand, contagion offers some diagnostic possibilities which might be summarized as Steele's Indirect Observation: *If we want to know what the major pathologies of the client group are, look at how we as a consulting team have changed since we started working with them. If we want to know what the major pathologies of our own team are, look at the ways in which the client group has become less effective since we started working with them.*

Of course, more direct observation of process problems is not ruled out. The point is simply that indirect observations can often suggest which process issues should be explored directly.

As to the source of contagion, the forces for this are from outside the consulting group (in the client → consultants direction). These forces are given impetus as they resonate with internal anxieties and disagreements within the team and its members and also by the general emotional stress of a task which requires confrontation, questioning, and dealing with feelings as well as ideas.

Splitting

The process of splitting takes its name from psychoanalytic theory, where splitting refers to the tendency of a patient to divide authority figures into two sharply distinguished groupings: those who are loving, good, nurturing, and generally like the "good" mother; and those who are overcontrolling, mean, harsh, and generally like the "bad" father. This stereotyping of authority figures into good and bad images is particularly likely to occur when two or more therapists are working within a group psychotherapy setting.

The point which is relevant to this chapter is that I have observed many instances of the same splitting process going on in a consulting situation where there are two or more consultants. The nature of the consulting task is such that the consultants will have to engage in a range of behaviors in order to be effective: they must be challenging at times, supportive at other times; rational and oriented toward solving problems at times, emotional and responsive to their own and others' feelings at other times. Clients tend to respond to this range of behaviors by splitting them into good and bad groupings and then projecting a relatively pure set onto a particular consultant. One consultant will be talked about by the client system as if he were consistently warm, supportive, and caring; while another will be described as always pushing, not caring, aggressive, hard, and so on.

My basic interpretation of this pattern is that the clients, when anxious about the uncertain outcomes of the change process, tend to reduce uncertainty by splitting the good and bad (emotional) aspects of the consulting team and perceiving them to reside in different people. This gives the clients clearer images of the consultants and a simpler choice of how to respond to each than if they saw the realities of the mixed character of each consultant.

I have been in each of these roles vis à vis a client group, and each has its costs for a consultant. The person who is seen as all bad, hostile, and demanding experiences quite a bit of stress; and he often cannot talk about that stress with a client group who consistently suspect his motives. On the other hand, if he is seen as all good, all loving, and the like, there are unreachable expectations placed on him. It also puts pressure on him not to confront, question, or generally use the more critical side of his faculties.

As already noted, the forces for splitting are from two main sources: the uncertainty of the task situation and its demands for a range of behaviors from the consultants, and the pressures from clients which they apply to the consultants in order to reduce their own anxieties about the uncertainties and risks of the change process.

Supersharpening

Along with the process of splitting, there is a related phenomenon which has its base in the internal responses of the consulting team itself. I call this *supersharpening,* and it refers to the tendency of consultants on a team to carve out private territories and become less and less like one another over the life of a project. The consultants become specialists in certain skills, styles, or whatever, even if in fact each has a rather broad range of things he can do. Here is one colleague's description of how he feels during the supersharpening process.

> Whenever I work with Jasper, I end up by not doing much with intrapersonal material of the group members. It's not that I can't do that sort of thing—I often do in other situations, and I'm pretty good at it. It's just that he does it so much and so well—and gets such a reverent response from the group for it—that I feel like that's his bag and I've got to stay away from it.

An interesting aspect of this is that I also talked with Jasper, who reported a similar feeling: when he works with the speaker, Jasper tends to work less on structural, process types of problems than he knows he is capable of doing. He feels that area is out of bounds for him, and that he gets reinforced by the group for sticking to what they see as the "real" Jasper. So each partner to the team tends to become a supersharpened version of himself, looking more like his strongest sides and staying away from other skills that could also be quite useful to the team and to the client system.

The root forces for supersharpening lie in both the internal relationships within the team, where lack of awareness of this process will tend to keep it operating, and in the input from the client system, when a consultant's "specialties" are overrewarded and his other skills get a cool or hostile reception. The obvious driving force which keeps supersharpening going is the individual consultant's need to experience himself as competent and effective in his professional role. Sticking to his "big number" is one way of reducing uncertainty about whether he will in fact make a difference in the current project.

One-Upmanship Spiral

While supersharpening allows for each person to be seen as competent in his own specialty, it still has some of the aspects of competition. Usually, the feeling is, "If I do that I won't look as good as Howard, so I'd better stay away from that area." It is possible though, for each consultant to pick a specialty and for them all to "win." With one-upmanship, however, the emphasis is directly on competition, and the game is defined by the need to have a winner and a loser.[5]

We all know that competitiveness can occur in any interpersonal situation, and it is not very startling to suggest that it can occur among consultants working as a team. It is the *spiral* aspect that I want to emphasize here. This is the process whereby, when one member of a team begins to feel less competent than another, each behaves in ways which tend to accentuate the "upness" of the one on top and the

5. Or as put by one-upmanship's creator, S. Potter, "He who is not one-up is one-down" (*Stephen Potter on Lifemanship* [London: Rupert Hart-Davis, 1950]).

"downness" of the one feeling less competent.[6] This creates a spiraling effect where the up-man gets further up and the down-man even more immersed in his feelings of incompetence and inability to act effectively. Rather than trying to reduce this feeling of tremendous differences in competence, the partners behave so as to accentuate it. As one colleague put it so well in an interview,

> when I'm going well and the clients are responding to all of what I do, I tend to trot out even more dazzling footwork and really turn on. I can feel myself swell with confidence, and it's like I'm buoyed up by a great swell of popular support. I can remember all sorts of things that will be likely to get at an issue. The person with me gets forgotten, I guess.
>
> On the other hand, I've also been in the one-down position. You see the other fellow with his fancy footwork, and the way the clients are responding to him, and you begin to feel that they'll never respond to *you* like that. I begin to get more tense, and that only makes it worse. Instead of confident, I begin to have feelings of doubt about whether I'm even in the right business in the first place. Instead of having this great mental storehouse to draw upon in the moment, I feel like I can't remember *anything* that would be worth doing. . . .

The forces which create one-upmanship spirals come from all three main sources. Obviously they are in part due to attitudes of competitiveness and evaluation on the part of team members toward one another. The spiral is helped along by the nature of the task, which often is ambiguous both in terms of the behavior which is called for at the moment and in terms of measures of whether that behavior was "successful" or not. The third component is clearly there as well, namely the responses and reinforcements of the client group. The clients can often make or break a consultant by what they are willing to do with his interventions, and to

6. Once again I am indebted to Barry Oshry for his help in clarifying this process.

some extent their perceptions of which consultants are competent tend to be self-fulfilling prophesies. They respond differentially to the inputs of the up-man and the down-man, and this gives the spiral a continuing nudge. A consultant who is one down often finds that it is true that he can do nothing "right," but it is because the clients also feel that he is one down and are unconsciously favoring the up-man.[7]

Stagnation

It seems to me that one of the most important features of a consultant's role is that he be engaged in a continuous learning process: learning about himself, about others, about the way social systems work, and about the ways in which change occurs and the ways he can help to effect that change. This is one of the most important potential outcomes of team consulting: that it provide an opportunity for rich learning experiences through feedback, conversation, and joint solving of problems among the consultants and clients. This also facilitates one of the most important goals of consulting, namely that the clients develop better learning styles themselves. A team of consultants who see their business as lifelong learning will also be modeling that stance for the clients.

Stagnation is the phenomenon which runs counter to these potentials. It simply refers to the situation in which a team has created a climate where they are no longer learning from one another. It comes in part from an overemphasis on performance as opposed to learning, a process which was discussed in chapter two. More generally, this climate can be said to exist when team members no longer give one another feedback, share opinions and ideas, or confront one another with intellectual or emotional differences.

There are several forces which push a consulting team toward a climate of stagnation. One is individual differences within the team. If there are too many wide differences of style and approach, team members gradually reduce their

7. This differential reinforcement is particularly visible with clients who take pride in being "good judges of men," and who are unaware of the role which they play in helping someone look good or bad.

inputs to one another because their experience tells them that it takes so much energy to work through to some common understanding. The opposite cause also has the same effect: if the members are all quite similar with too few differences, controversy and discussion tend to die out for lack of useful differing positions. Another internal force is the competitive spirit which was discussed above. If people feel evaluative and competitive with one another, they are less likely to allow themselves to be observed and to accept feedback as useful input. They tend to overmanage instances where a competitor can observe them in action. In training laboratories, this often leads to each trainer carefully guarding and nurturing the growth of his own T-group, with very little cross-group contact or joint involvement in learning for the staff.

The pressures of the task also add to a tendency toward stagnation. It is easy in an ambiguous and demanding task situation to fill up the team's time with "essential" activities which must take a higher priority than reflection, sharing of experiences, and other means of helping one another learn. The doing tends to drive out processing types of activities. Pressures from the client amplify this tendency, especially if the client does not share the consultants' values about learning as a continuous process. Other role demands also compete for time and energy and create a conflict which is usually resolved in favor of the demandant at the expense of the learning of the person on whom the demands are made.

Overprocessing

The last pathology I shall deal with here is, in a sense, the mirror image of stagnation. It is over-processing, the tendency of a consulting team to spend so much time and energy on processing experiences, internal problems, et cetera, that they are immobilized and are unable to take any kind of real action in the client system. In chapter four I referred to this as the "congenital" problem of a consulting organization. Since consultants' business is dealing with structure and process and learning from it, they tend to apply this skill with a vengeance within the system as well as to the clients. By and large this is as it should be, but it can become exaggerated and no longer be a choice which the team is making. Here are samples of notes I made while observing one consulting group.

> It seems clear now that they are stuck on the kick of processing every innuendo or possible meaning that could be gotten out of every statement in the team. It has a little of the quality of masturbation, since I can't see how it has made much difference to their functioning as a group. . . . In this instance, a couple of them ought to be with Hugh [a client system manager] while he explains the program, rather than where they are, sitting here discussing one another.

The point is not that processing of internal issues is not useful, only that it must be done out of choice, not compulsion, and it must be integrated with action in the client system so that it can lead to real learning, not to mere following of a form which has no solid data input from which learning can occur. The forces for overprocessing tend to come from the ambiguous nature of the task, the stresses of having to react on the spot when with the client, and anxieties over whether anything useful is being done. In addition, individual consultants' training can push them in this direction, especially if there are undercurrents of competition in the group as to who can be the most sensitive, most oriented toward process, and so on. When overprocessing occurs, it becomes a ritualized demonstration of competence and has little solid outcome in terms of the members learning anything. Consultants who are caught up in overprocessing tend to do what they already know how to do best, not to experiment with new ideas, feelings, or behaviors.

The Effective Consulting Team Process

To summarize very briefly, there are three main sources of forces on consulting team relationships: forces from within the team, from outside the team, and from the characteristics of the task of effecting change. These forces are useful in providing inputs and mobilizing the team to effective action. They also carry the seeds of a number of pathological processes which limit the effectiveness and development of both consultants and clients. The pathologies used here as illustrations were discontinuity, vectorization, contagion, splitting, supersharpening, one-upmanship spirals, stagnation, and overprocessing.

The next question is, What can be done to deal with these pathologies? How can we build a collaborative consulting team which tends toward healthy processes and effective action with the client system? Although there are no firmly established "rules" for a consulting team any more than there are for work groups in general, I believe that we do know a good deal about what tends to make a consulting team most effective and healthy. I believe we can identify some of the major features of a nonpathological consulting team. Most of them are criteria that we as consultants apply to client systems, and I am merely highlighting the fact that they must be applied to the consulting team as well. The suggestions fall into four major areas: social invention, openness, self-conscious research, and mixed teams.

Social Invention

One of the most important concepts to emerge from behavioral science consulting is, in my opinion, the notion of *social invention*. This is simply the realization that social settings do not have to be taken only as they occur by chance. Rather, if a certain kind of social event or grouping of people is needed, it is possible to consciously design it and cause it to happen. This may seem like an obvious point, but the history of the world is filled with examples of persons who took the tide and events as they came, and it is underrepresented by persons who made events happen.

The point to be made for consulting teams is that it is very easy to drift along from day to day without very much conscious influence over the ways people get together within the team. Even while encouraging the client system to take a greater hand in its own fate, the consultant team is often doing the opposite, leading to the pathologies described above. These may be occurring regularly, and yet no concrete steps are taken to relieve them.

What are some of the areas which can be approached through more conscious social invention within the team? One is definition of and assignment to a role. Being explicit about the particular functions which members are playing within the client system helps relieve the tendencies toward supersharpening, splitting, and one-upmanship spirals. Conscious choices about roles make client response a more legitimate area for *joint* discussion, and they help to keep an individual consultant from sinking into a wallow of self-deprecation where he feels sure that his inadequacy is the real cause of a problematical situation.

A second area for invention is concerned with long- and short-term planning on a project. The more this is done explicitly and periodically, with built-in checkpoints, the less likely discontinuity and vectorization are to occur. A colleague can then challenge inappropriate neutralizing behaviors without the challenge being seen as simply coming from competitive or jealous feelings. If planning is built-in, then steps will be checked for whether they aid or block the general trend of the plan.

A crucial area of invention is related to the problem of stagnation. Stagnation tends to occur because either activities are blocking learning or people are not providing inputs for one another. Both of these processes can be alleviated by design of specific events which are aimed toward learning. Forums for specific value issues in consulting should be a part of every team's process. Clinic sessions on a particular client or problem situation should be, too. Care must be taken to design sessions at points in time where they can be most useful, for example, when good data about a change project are available rather than before the data are perceivable or usable. It also helps to structure the sessions so that everyone understands that the main purpose is *learning,* rather than evaluation, demonstration of superior competence, solving problems, or whatever. As I will discuss below, these other forces will be present in any event that has a task as threatening as consciously attempting to learn from one's consulting experiences; and it takes considerable commitment to learning, to one another, and to looking at the group's process to keep these other forces from becoming dominant.

My broadest suggestion about social invention is simply that it is limited only by the team's ability to think up new temporary structures. Almost any problem has some event or grouping of people which would enable the data about the problem to get into the open and be worked through. The main requirement for doing this is a commitment on the consultants' part to be creative about *their own* social structures (not just the clients') and to actually try out their inventions.

Openness

There seems to me to be no substitute for openness on a consulting team. By openness I mean communication in two directions: a willingness to *disclose* what you are thinking and feeling, and an equal willingness to *receive* new information, opinions, feelings, and the like. An effective open climate means both of these, since neither is as valuable alone as they are together. Carl Rogers put it well with his notion that "the facts are friendly" (1960, p. 25), by which he meant that in the long run your purposes are better served by dealing with reality than not, even though you may feel otherwise at any given moment.

For the disclosure side of the process, it is very important that consultants be willing to share thoughts and feelings with one another, particularly in the area of how they are working together. This is usually a process goal which the consultants have for the client system, yet it is all too easy to forget it in dealing with one another as collaborators. The risks of disclosure are also high at times, so it is not just a problem of memory.

For example, a consultant who feels himself on the low side of a one-upmanship spiral will shy away from raising the question, because it may put him even more one-down. I have been in this position and have felt that it would make me look even clumsier to say anything. Yet the opposite is usually true. If it is indeed a collaborative relationship, then the fact that you are feeling one-down is a *joint* problem for both you and the up-man, not just *your* problem. If there is a joint commitment to what the team is producing, then the spiral must be examined, since it is neutralizing half of the resources of the team. The same is true for processes such as splitting, supersharpening, and discontinuity. Whoever spots them must be willing to raise the question of their appearance, if he is going to reduce their negative effects even though he risks looking foolish at the start. This type of disclosure obviously requires that there be a minimum level of basic trust and commitment between the team members. This trust will then serve as a counterweight to the feelings of competition, foolishness, and anxiety which a person may experience at a particular moment.

On the receiving side, I know of no better way for disclosure to fall off over time than when the receivers are not open to hearing what the discloser is saying or doing. It seems to me to be a vital characteristic of a consulting team and its members that they be open to new ways of looking at problems and to hearing notions which at first may not seem very comfortable. The task of consulting is too fluid and demanding to allow for rock-solid formulas to be developed and carried out by rote. This fluidity therefore requires an open stance which promotes the examination of new information, assumptions, and possibilities.

Taken together, high disclosure and high receptivity allow teams to correct their own process, to not be captives of external inputs, and to be masters of their own fate. When a syndrome such as splitting is developing, and consultants are being differentially reinforced by the clients, an ability to deal openly with the issue can short-circuit the splitting cycle. If this ability is not there, the splitting process can neutralize all of the consultants, as well as turn them against one another.

Openness is also one of the most important means of avoiding stagnation. If persons cannot talk with one another about their experiences, assumptions, and reactions in different situations, it is very difficult for them to learn from one another. Each tends to believe that his assumptions are descriptions of the external world without thinking that they are also products of his particular internal state. If events occur in a consultation, and people do not share openly their observations and reactions, it is difficult to ever see the pattern of the total process, since each participant has only a part of the picture. True learning demands that people pool their resources, but this means that they be willing to both throw them in the pool and pull out the things that others have thrown in.

Another issue for consultants is *where* to be open. There is a continuing question in consulting of how open consultants can be with one another in front of clients. The argument for a closed attitude toward team members when the client is present usually stresses the anxieties which open confrontation between consultants would raise in the clients. The clients want to see the consulting team as experts in agreement on direction and method and generally as an integrated source of authority. The opposing argument suggests that openness and dealing with live issues are exactly the skills which most client systems tend to lack, and this is why the human side of their system is not so effective as it could be. Given this, if the consultants do not behave openly with one another, they tend, as Argyris (1961) has pointed out, to reinforce the very processes which they are trying to change.

I am personally more convinced by the second position than by the first. I believe that I have moved further, often quite rapidly, with a client when I have been open with colleagues in front of him. He has gotten a bit of a live model of what we have often been talking about only theoretically. In addition, he sees us as human beings who have a variety of styles and reaction, rather than simply as members of a team. Being perceived as human beings gets us closer to the realities of the consulting situation. Finally, the research by Gladstone and Burkham (1966) cited earlier suggests that when team members are not open with each other in front of a client, the disagreements get transmitted in more subtle ways, through cues such as how the consultants speak to one another, how quickly they follow each other, and how much they engage in vectorization. The client gets a sense that there *are* differences, but he gets no direct data as to their nature or how they are resolved. This means that he can neither play a part in the resolution process (and I believe he should, since it involves him), nor can he learn from observing how it is managed. This seems to me to be a waste of the process skills for which the consultants were brought to the project in the first place.

Self-conscious Research

Another means for keeping the pathologies described in this chapter from becoming ingrained in the team is to be continuously involved in research on the process of the team itself. This should be a regular, systematic set of mechanisms for collecting data about the individuals, relationships, and processes by which the consulting team is functioning, as well as about the resulting effects on the client system.

Traditionally in consulting the emphasis on the research side has been on gathering data about the clients, not the consultants. When the clients have balked at research, no research at all has been done. As I wrote in the *Journal of Applied Behavioral Science:*

There are clearly other possibilities which would not require intrusion into a skittish client world. For instance, the consultants could design data-collection instruments for *themselves,* to look at their behavior under different conditions, how they resolved team conflicts, strategy choices, and the forces that influenced these choices. . . . It may be that for many consultants/researchers, talking about the client's resistance to research is a way of externalizing and not having to own our own mixed feelings about being under scrutiny in situations where we feel clumsy. I know I have felt this myself and used it as a rationale for not collecting more systematic data. It does make me suspicious when I say, "Well, we certainly can't study *them*," and then forget about asking whether we can study *us*. [1970, p. 362]

I am suggesting an alternative stance which consulting teams could use to great benefit: a continuing data collection on themselves. This requires a willingness to put energy into social inventions which will generate data. Some which I have tried are using consultants as process observers for one another, using outside observers to study our process in team meetings and in contact with the client system, video and audio tapings which allow us repeated access to raw data about how we were functioning, reaction scales which the consultants fill out during a team session, scales for the client to fill out after contact with the consultants, and diaries kept by consultants and clients recording events and feelings related to the change process. I am sure there are many others which could be devised as well.

The effective use of these mechanisms requires that consultants be willing to look at the less-than-perfect aspects of themselves. As I indicated in the above quote, this is not always easy, especially for people whose business is helping in the improvement of *other* people. Professional helpers are often the last to feel comfortable with the process of being helped or observed by somebody else. Besides commitment to learning, a climate of true openness is required, so that people will level about how they saw one another and what kinds of issues they felt concerned about as a result of observing a particular event.

If the commitment to learning is there, a climate of openness exists, and the team puts some energy into inventing means of gathering continuous data about themselves, then it is much less likely that any of the pathologies described earlier could develop and become permanent fixtures. They are bound to occur at different points in the consultation, but they can be spotted and dealt with before they become ingrained and overly destructive of the change process and the team itself.

Mixed Teams

My final means for maintaining a healthy consulting team is concerned with the make-up of the team itself. The nature of skills, styles, and personal needs which a team possesses is a major factor in its susceptibility to the various pathologies. For instance, a team with members who are all similar in style and theoretical outlook will be one where stagnation is more likely to occur than in a more mixed team. Similarly, a team made up of people who all need a great deal of reassurance about competence and/or connectedness is likely to fall into the overprocessing mode. They are also more likely to be subject to contagion from the client's symptoms, since they will tend to have similar feelings about the clients' problems. On the other hand, a team with members who are extremely different from one another may get locked into one-upmanship spirals, discontinuity cycles, and vectorization, so that they may never develop any real thrust as a group. They also find it difficult to learn, since they reject each others' positions too quickly.

These observations suggest that a curvilinear relationship is present, and that an effective consulting team is one which has differences of styles and viewpoint represented, but not such great gaps that there is little possibility of developing shared goals and understandings.

A Final Observation on Mixtures

Another issue is raised by the last discussion of the mixture in a team. This is the question of what theoretical or academic disciplines are represented. What kinds of training have been acquired by the team members? Another pathology might have been included in the earlier list, one which we could call *insularity*. By this I mean the tendency for consulting teams to form around a particular discipline and to subsequently exclude other areas. Behavioral science consultants are particularly prone to do this, I believe, mainly because of their tendency to see change problems in purely behavioral terms. General management consultants also do this, as do city planning consultants, computer sciences experts, lawyers, and so on. The point is that the exponent of each area, if it alone is represented on a team, tends to see the client's problems in his own terms and to feel more and more that only his viewpoint can solve these problems.

In fact, any complex social system usually has problems which are an interlocking function of several of these areas. I believe that the most important development which will take place in consulting in the coming years is the formation of teams with a greater mixture of trained areas and skills. This is the only way that systematic change services which really make a long-term difference will be provided to a client system. I have been attempting one step in this direction through combining physical design of organizations with behavioral organization development strategies. These are two obvious areas which interact with one another in their impact on the system but have traditionally been handled independently (see Steele, 1973).

The greater the mixture of disciplines on a consulting team, the more exaggerated its pathologies may become. Many factors contribute to this: differences in world-view, in working language, in time scales for expected change, and in conceptions of role, such as the use of power versus that of experimentation. All these differences help create process problems, and this makes all the more critical the notion of continuing attention to the actual workings of the team itself, as opposed to simply talking about the clients' problems. This is also a great challenge to behavioral science members of a team: to help this examination process without getting locked into a one-upmanship spiral or supersharpening process where other team members reject group self-analysis as simply the behavioral scientists trying to impose their "thing" on everyone else.

This chapter would best be closed where it started, with the unfortunate lack of specific data about the collaborative process in consultation. The discussion is really no more than a beginning look at the problems involved in teamwork on change. Issues such as the difference between teams external to a client system and teams internal to the system have not been touched upon, nor has the question of how external teams collaborate and compete with one another. Many of the observations I have made need much more systematic verification. I hope that the ideas I have discussed here will be a stimulus for a great deal more work on the demands and possibilities of team consultation.

8. Consultants and Detectives

Introduction

The previous chapters have described examples of different modes of gaining insight into the opportunities and dilemmas of the consulting process. Some of the ideas have been theoretical, others had their origin in live consulting experiences, and still others were the result of experiences in laboratory training sessions.

This chapter's mode of analysis does not quite fit any of these. It stems instead from observations of myself wasting time. After years of avidly reading the British detective novels of such authors as Dorothy Sayers, Margery Allingham, Michael Innes, and the like, it occurred to me that the same personal characteristics which draw me to consulting work may determine the form taken by my flight-relaxation behavior. This in turn suggested to me that we may, by examining activities other than those connected with consulting per se, be able to discover some of the more subtle attributes and dilemmas connected with the consultant's role.

In this chapter I demonstrate this process by a comparison of the similarities in the roles of the consultant and the classic British detective. Although I have chosen to focus attention on my interest in British detectives, there are obviously many other attributes which might be looked at: preferences for social gatherings and interpersonal encounters of one

A shorter version of this chapter appeared in the *Journal of Applied Behavioral Science* 5, no. 2 (1969): 187–202. Reproduced by special permission from *Journal of Applied Behavioral Science*. Copyright © 1969 by NTL Institute for Applied Behavioral Science.

sort or another, interest in various sports, activities in the arts, and so on. Many of these might be worth exploring for the same kinds of analogies which will be discussed here.

Comparing the Two Roles

The format will be a rather basic listing and discussion of some of the major similarities which I see between the role of the organizational consultant and the role of the British detective. I should emphasize here a fundamental point: there are obviously many different styles and kinds of organizational consultants, and the analogies I will be making will depend to a great extent on my own personal view of what a consultant does. Also, when I use the term *consultant* here, I am referring to those consultants who are specifically oriented toward changing the structure or behavior of the client system through application of behavioral science knowledge. I do not consider specifically other types of consultants, such as market research firms, which provide services related to the actual tasks of the organization itself.

The Focus on Evidence

Clearly, one of the major activities of the detective is an extensive search for clues and evidence as to what has occurred in a specific situation. Quite often this evidence is fleeting and must be gathered as it passes, as in the following example from Marsh.

> Alleyn moved forward. He noticed as he did so that Peregrine stationed himself beside Miss Emily Dunne, that there was a glint of fanaticism in the devouring stare that Jeremy Jones bent upon the glove, that Winter Meyer expanded as if he had some proprietary rights over it and that Emily Dunne appeared to unfold a little at the approach of Peregrine. [1966, p. 142]

The detective's reason for wanting evidence may be described as falling into two major categories: one need is to gather clues to help him to *understand* what has occurred in a given criminal situation, and a second need concerns using that understanding to search out more adequate evidence in order to *prove to others* what has occurred and make a case which can stand up in court. Both of these seems to me to be of vital importance to the consultant as well. A consultant who focuses attention on active intervention in an organization must be continually seeking to understand the data with which he comes into contact. And it is of great value to collect and organize these data in such a way as to provide clear, straightforward evidence to the client system supporting the points which he will use in trying to bring about change in the system.

It has been my experience that this building up of a pool of evidence which is clear and can be seen in a relatively undistorted way by the client system is a very important focal point for the consultant who wishes to guide an organization in the direction of greater acceptance of reality. In other words, just *telling* a client system where it ought to go because of a theory which one has about how organizations ought to operate is not really enough. The consultant must be able to present a very good case for where the organization is, what the consequences of its present position are, and some of the major factors which keep it in that particular position. He should also strive to build *within* the client system the capacity and inclination to *continually* collect evidence of what is going on so they can make cases to themselves.

Considering this focus on evidence apart from questions of effective performance, I also recognize in myself a strong emotional attachment to the process of trying to solve challenging puzzles. This is probably one of the clearest of the common attributes which draw me to both the detective novel and the consulting process. I obviously share this love of puzzles with Dickson's Sir Henry Merrivale:

> Sudden inspiration seemed to distend H.M.'s cheeks, like an ogre in a pantomime. Breaking open the magazine, which showed the ends of cartridge cases, he plucked out

one bullet. He scrutinized it carefully, also weighing it in his hand. He did this, while Cy's nerves ached, with every bullet in the magazine; and shut it up again.

"So!" he repeated, dropping the revolver on the floor with an echoing clatter of marble. "Don't you see what this place means now?" [1951, p. 141]

As I will discuss below, the love of puzzles for their own sake can at times be a diversion for the consultant from the needs of the client, especially when the consultant gets wrapped up in demonstrating his ability to unravel the puzzle.

Temporary Involvement

Another characteristic of the British detective is his temporary involvement in a system or group of people. He establishes a network of relationships for the duration of the case. He may be quite central to several of these relationships, and they may be very important at the time, but then he generally moves on to a new set. The network of relationships in the detective story implies a sense of impermanence and some psychological distance. The detective acquires a kind of credibility without permanent closeness.[1] Here is Allingham's Albert Campion settling into a new scene for the first time, a place which will be the locus of a number of startling events.

Mr. Campion appeared to have been forgotten, and he sat in a little recess in a corner of the hall and looked through the open doorway at the quivering leaves and dancing water without. The old house seemed very quiet after the hullabaloo. It was really amazingly attractive. Like all very old houses it had a certain drowsy elegance that was soothing and comforting in a madly gyrating world. [1950, p. 71]

1. This is similar to the notion of temporary structures which Bennis sees as being a central characteristic of organizations of the future (1966, p. 12).

Campion is at the same time establishing a relationship with the family who lives in the house, and for the duration of the mystery, they and the house are his world.

I find myself strongly drawn toward this temporary kind of involvement with a group of people, and I gather from my contacts with other consultants that many of them do also. This seems to be a seductive characteristic which often intrigues the client system members as well, and they often speak longingly of the consultants' chances to use a variety of settings and engage in a variety of activities day to day. However, this orientation can also have some costs. It may serve as flight from necessary deep involvement in and working through a particular problem, and this may either reduce the clients' willingness to provide important data or impair the consultant's ability to understand the situation. I am sure that there are moments for both the detective and the consultant when each would like to take the earliest opportunity to get out out of the system, because things are getting too close or unmanageable. However, as I see it, each has a certain innate basic curiosity or desire to be competent which leads him generally to stay with a particular case or problem or to terminate the relationship because of a prediction of little likelihood of further change (rather than termination simply because of a need to move on).

Another side of the question of involvement concerns the power which a system has over someone who is trying to change it. In the case of a detective the system generally has little or no power over him, including the decision whether he is to be there or not. In the case of the consultant the system has only limited power, chiefly in that area of decisions related to whether the consultant should continue in a relationship with the client (a power which the consultant shares). In this sense, then, a consultant is intermediate (in terms of freedom of action) between the detective and the internal members of a system, such as internal agents of change. This in turn suggests that serving as an *internal* consultant carries with it a need for some important assumptions, such as a willingness to test the degrees of freedom one has, or a willingness to try to increase those degrees of freedom.

Incorporation into the System

One of the forces which is often at work on the British detective is related to his relative independence of a given group. There is usually a series of attempts by the persons with whom he is involved to incorporate him into the group. He is a real threat to that particular group of people, and they attempt to neutralize his threat to them by drawing him inside their boundaries as best they can. Here is another example from Allingham, where Campion's protagonist is attempting to win him over.

> As he sat down again he [Campion] noticed that the other had undergone a complete change of mood. His bullying vanished and seemed to have decided to become hearty.
>
> "Well, my boy," he said, "so you've come about the papers. Rather good that eh? It sounded interesting. Didn't give anything away. Now, I've been hearing a good deal about you, one way and another, and I've sent for you because I think I can put something your way that may interest you."
>
> Mr. Campion peered round the corner of his handkerchief.
>
> "Very nice of you, as long as it isn't a spoke in my wheel," he murmured idiotically. [1950, p. 122]

The point is that I have had more than one very similar conversation with a company executive at about the time during a project that it began to look as though real change might occur. I believe that the consultant is subject to the same kinds of forces and for the same reasons: he represents a certain threat to the client system, possibly one that has not even been consciously considered by the individuals involved. However, their way of dealing with the threat which he raises is to try to swallow him, in a figurative sense, by making him a permanent part of the system and thereby increasing the system's power over him. Almost every consultant with whom I am associated can call to mind numerous instances of the client system's attempt to incorporate him and make him a permanent resident of that system. One reason for this may relate to his perceived competence and his abilities, which could be of great value for a long term to the group; but I am convinced that at least a large part of this need stems from the threat, which may be unnamed, to the clients themselves. In sociological terms, this is similar to the process of attempted "co-optation" into a system.

Intuition

The British detective often uses intuition as a mode of operation. He generates hypotheses from within, which he then attempts to test by either gathering new data or by sifting through the old data again. He often does not know for a considerable length of time why he is looking at a particular corner of the data pile, but his intuition keeps him there until the connections get made. Consider this description of Gideon from Marric.

> "Just tell me what it's all about and I'll tell you what I can." Gideon did not know why he evaded the question as he did; there was something of a sixth sense in his move, that sense which made him so much more able than most detectives. He knew that Abbott would not interrupt or give him away, and he said: "She's been missing since Wednesday evening." [1963, p. 63]

I think that the intuitive mode is also a very important one for consultants. I find that sometimes I almost stop trying to control *where* I focus my attention and let natural awareness lead me in whatever direction it will. In a sense, I try to stop staring (looking hard without really seeing) at the data and allow the figure and ground relationships to shift around and take on new meanings or new potencies for me. I do not believe that a consultant can do this without some intuition, some way to generate contextual notions so that he can understand what it is he sees as he lets his eye and mind roam over the situation.

One bit of evidence for intuition as an important process for consultants is presented in a study I made (1968b). I found that laboratory trainers had a high mean score on the sensation-intuition scale of the Myers-Briggs Type Indicator. The trainers' mean was 135, compared with 98.7 for a sample from middle management; the higher the score on this scale, the stronger the indication of preference for intuition as a means of becoming aware of things, that is, for generating possibilities from within as well as using data obtained through the senses.

By stressing intuition here, I am not suggesting that the detective and the consultant do not put a very large amount of energy into purposeful plans, logically aimed thinking, or follow-up, but only that a too quick focusing in on what are "obviously" the major elements in the case or the problem situation may lead to staring. This in turn can create an inability to see new relationships which may, in fact, be more important than the first ones that come to mind.

A Sense of the Dramatic

The British detective likes to be at center stage and to control the timing of events. He often works very carefully to choose just the right time for certain actions, sometimes as much for effect and his own personal centrality as for any other reason connected with accomplishing the case. Agatha Christie's Hercule Poirot is a good example, as are those two rotund rooters-out of crime, Sir Henry Merrivale:

> H.M., as usual, was basking in the spotlight. In response to the cheers he first bowed, then he lifted both hands above his head and shook hands with himself, like a prize fighter entering the ring. [Dickson 1951, p. 116]

and Dr. Gideon Fell:

> Now, then, excuse the old charlatan a moment. I am going to make some telephone-calls. Not under torture would I reveal what I intend to do, or where's the fun of mystifying

you, hey? Hey! There's no pleasure like mystification, my boy, if you can pull it off. . . . [Carr 1962, p. 145]

I know I can sense within myself at times this same wish to be in the center of an unfolding drama. I suspect that I make more choices to create this situation than I like to think I do. There are times in group settings where I think I do something dramatic, and it is for at least two reasons: one is the perception on my part that confrontation at a particular moment will help to shake up the situation and bring a bit more data to the surface, and the other is that I like the image of myself as one who confronts. I think I like to engage in some behaviors which are seen by the clients as beyond the bounds of what they would do but still within their definition of what is dramatic, unusual, and exciting, with a certain flair.

I am calling attention to this need to be dramatic, because I think there are times when it can get in the way of effective consultation if it is not tested for its value as an intervention. The more dazzling the footwork of the actor, the less the members of the audience are aware of themselves. In consultation, this focus of attention on the consultant may block the clients' awareness of how central *they* must be in the drama of unfolding organizational change, and it may actually decrease self-awareness instead of increase it. It can also lead the clients to a definition of the situation such that most of the responsibility for change, innovation, and creation of excitement lies in the consultant rather than in themselves.

The Expert

Just as the detective-consultant's dramatic *actions* may cause the client's attention to focus too completely on the consultant, the same effect may also be brought about by idealized perceptions of the consultant's *knowledge* in a particular problematical situation. The detective has a tendency to unfold little of his reasoning prior to the climax of a case, and the more he does this, the more likely he is to appear omniscient in the end if he gets the pieces together (for either the right or the wrong reasons). This is another of Sir Henry's favorite tricks:

> "Look here," said Cy, and drank a cup of cold coffee. "Why in blazes can't you just tell us? . . . Yes, yes, I know!" he added hastily, as H.M. began to draw himself up, "you're the old man! We understand that. All the same, can't you give us an idea?"
>
> "I told you last night," H.M. pointed out, "that Manning's trick was based on the same principle I used myself when I hocussed the subway turnstiles."
>
> "And that tells me a hell of a lot, doesn't it?" [Dickson 1951, p. 215]

I think the role of "expert" is a quite seductive one for the consultant; all the more so in behavioral science, since the variables and their relationships are often very fuzzy and complex. It can be quite personally gratifying to have others see me as someone who really "knows" what is going on or what should be done in a given situation. Besides personal gratification on the part of the consultant, another factor pushes him toward the stance of expert: the client's wish to see himself safely in the hands of an expert who is wise and able, so that anxiety over present or future difficulties can be reduced.

Both the consultant's and the client's needs, then, may propel the consultant toward exclusive occupancy of the role of expert in their relationship. This may have some benefits, such as making it more likely that the consultant will be listened to, but it also has some costs. One that is usually mentioned is the potential price in terms of increased dependency of the client on the consultant, a dependency which may keep the client from developing his own strengths and competences for the diagnosis and solving of problems. A second cost, one which is less often considered, is that a reliance on the consultant as the exclusive expert may often lead to inadequate decisions. The client often has great wisdom (intuitive if not systematic) about many aspects of his own situation, and an overweighting of the value placed on the consultant's knowledge may indeed cause poorer choices to be made than if there were a more balanced view of what each can contribute to the situation.[2]

Who Are the Suspects?

Another characteristic of the detective's role is the necessity of his considering all possibilities regarding those whom he should suspect in a given case. This means that he tends to consider all people as possible culprits, including both those who seem to be the most innocent and those who seem to be the most guilty. The former category may often include the very people who called the detective onto the case in the beginning. Consider this reaction from the member of a theater company being interviewed by Inspector Alleyn after a murder:

> "Who's going to pitch into me next?" he asked. "I ought to be getting hospital attention, the shock I've had, and not subjected to what'd bring about an inquiry if I made complaints. I ought to be home in bed getting looked after."
>
> "So you shall be," Alleyn said. "We'll send you home in style when you've just told me quietly what happened."
>
> "I have! I have told. I've told them others."
>
> "All right. I know you're feeling rotten and it's a damn shame to keep you but you see you're the chap we're looking to for help."
>
> "Don't you use that yarn to me. I know what the police mean when they talk about help. Next thing it'll be the Usual Bloody Warning." [Marsh 1966, p. 155]

Imagine how much help Alleyn will get from him in his present mood of mistrust. But his feeling is well founded, for at the moment Alleyn needs his help and simultaneously

2. This view of the price paid by ignoring the innate wisdom of the client was clarified for me in a conversation with Edgar Schein.

must consider the possibility that he actually is the guilty person masquerading behind his hurt feelings.

In a very similar manner, the consultant must stay open to all possibilities in terms of who may be the "culprits" in a given problem. This means that he considers suspect even those persons who originally invited him into the system. By "suspects," in this instance, I mean people who may contribute in some significant way to difficulties or problem situations. Interestingly enough, the members of the client organization often seem to feel very similar to the suspects in a detective case, particularly if they do not know exactly what line of thought the consultant is taking. They have a fear of being "caught," even when they do not know at *what* they may be "caught." The analogue in the organization to a crime in the detective novel seems to be being ineffective or doing something which is not seen by the consultant or persons in positions of power as leading to productivity or success in the organization. Using this definition, it has been my experience that almost everyone in a client system seems to feel that the consultant may uncover some "crime" which he has committed in the past or is committing at present. It is no surprise, then, that members of a client system often exhibit many of the same characteristics of uneasiness or mistrust toward a consultant that suspects in a detective case exhibit toward the investigator.

One of the consequences of this mistrust or uneasiness is the withholding or distortion of information which is vital to an understanding of the problem situation. This obviously makes the task of understanding and changing a system just that much more difficult and, at times, impossible. This implies that a key task of the consultant would be to help people stop defining themselves as culprits, that is, to change their view of less-than-perfectly-effective behavior from criminal to human and to redefine change as a continuing process of improvement, rather than a weeding out of antisocial elements.

This redefinition should probably start with the consultant's view of his own process. I think it is all too easy for a consultant to emotionally respond to members of the client system as if they, based on their willingness to change, were two distinct groups, the Goodies and the Baddies, and to treat them so that the Baddies *do* get the impression that they are criminals to be hunted down. This can be very self-defeating behavior on our part if the guilt we induce in the Baddies cannot be dealt with and resolved, and it may also create in the Goodies a sense of having "succeeded" to the point of closing them to an awareness of needed changes in their behavior. In addition, even the Goodies are not outside the limitations of the crime-and-punishment set of assumptions; when a consultant does confront them with some data he feels they should consider, they often feel that a "surprise arrest" has been made when they least expected it, and this can make their resistance to considering the possibility of change just as high as that of the so-called Baddies.

Action Intervention

One characteristic of the style of a number of fictional detectives with whom I am familiar is a precipitation of specific planned events which the detective predicts will produce an imbalance in the situation. This imbalance then causes someone to react, to take further action, which then provides more information about the total situation which the detective is trying to understand. This reaction helps the detective in diagnosing what the major forces are in the problem situation, helps him to understand better the orientations of the other individuals involved, and creates forces for change in the situation. Here for example, is another instance of Albert Campion stirring the pot:

> "But consider, my dear old flag-wagger, how on earth do you imagine this beautiful soul down here [a crook] ever heard about the oak? He heard about it because little Albert sent him a note with 'Look what I've found in the mill loft, Ducky', or words to that effect, neatly written above my usual signature." [Allingham 1950, p. 37]

In this instance, Campion sensed that the best way to find out what the man wanted was to hold out some opportunity for him to get it.

This action-reaction process is very similar to Lewin's suggestion that if you want to understand something, a good approach is to try to change it. It seems to me that one of the reasons why I intervene in a system (such as in confronting someone), as well as affecting that system in some way which I think may be positive, is also just to find out more about the system. In the same way that the detective may obtain some expected or unexpected results from his intervention, I often think that the consultant may gather a large portion of his data by actually doing things: by acting in the system itself. For me, it is this orientation toward action which makes the temporary involvement which I mentioned earlier a palatable one, and this may be true for other consultants as well.

There is another side to this question of action, however. As I thought about it, it dawned on me why I am using *British* detectives, and not American, as my role comparison. It is because there is less action for action's sake alone in the British detective stories. Rather, there is a mixture of contemplation, detection, and action which I find more appealing than the more violent American novels. The parallel to consulting is clear here: I am suggesting that at times it may be quite important that the consultant *not* engage in action for action's sake, particularly since this often seems to be one part of the clients' value system which is getting them into some of their difficulties. As Argyris (1961) has pointed out, engaging in some behavior simply because it fits the clients' expectation or value system may in fact limit the usefulness of the consultant to the client.

Self-Consciousness

A very important characteristic related to taking action in a system is self-consciousness about one's action. This is reflected in the detective's attempts to really step outside himself and look at himself as if he were someone else observing him in action. Here is Alleyn in a "processing session" with himself:

> He could have kicked himself from Whitehall to Blankside. Why, why, why, hadn't he put his foot down about the safe and its silly window and bloody futile combination lock? Why hadn't he said that he would on no account recommend it? He reminded himself that he had given sundry warnings but snapped back at himself that he should have gone further. [Marsh 1966, p. 151]

The tendency toward self-examination obviously varies with the detectives involved, but I think that it sheds a great light on a key demand of the consultant role.[3] To me, this self-consciousness needs to be a central characteristic of the consultant's functioning, similar to its importance for the psychoanalyst and psychotherapist. This is because the consultant is serving as a data-gathering instrument (mainly trying to become aware of the data in the situation but also trying to understand how he is "calibrated"), and he himself is also one of the major inputs, causing reactions in the system as he is diagnosing, intervening, et cetera. As such, he must be able to have a sense of who and what he is, what he represents to the client system, what actions he is taking, and whether he can accept them or not.

I find this to be one of the most interesting, most compelling, and most difficult aspects of the role. It requires a great deal of discipline to keep one's self from throwing away three-quarters of the relevant data. By this I mean that so many of the important things having to do with the consultant's own process in a given situation are so close to him and so much a part of him that it is very difficult for him to see them. He therefore has to be willing to take a look at himself in terms of dimensions which he may consider to be almost self-evident, such as the ways he feels when he is about to contact the client, or the method he chooses when he does it. Many of these kinds of data may have important

3. The most notable examples with which I am familiar are Tey's Inspector Grant, Simenon's Maigret, and Marric's Commander Gideon.

implications for the consultant-client relationship and for needed changes in the consultant's behavior.

Collaboration

Perhaps the above considerations are some of the reasons why most of the British detectives seem to have some sort of partner with whom they can talk, get new ideas and energy, relieve tension, or just speak the same language.[4] They are generally people who have worked with the detective in the past, and they often refer to other cases and their similarities to the present one. This may serve as a good advertising mechanism for the author, but in terms of the relationship between the detective and his sidekick, it also seems to signal to each other that they speak a common language, that they understand each other and think along the same dimensions, and that they thereby share a closeness which is lacking in the detective's relationships with others in the case.

As I noted in the preceding chapter, it is very important to have an associate in the organizational consulting process. It seems to me that there is a clear need on the part of someone who is dealing with ambiguous data, difficult emotional issues, and a relatively new field, to have someone who speaks his language so that he can discuss problems, issues, and just general feelings of frustration, anxiety, and elation. I know this is true for me, and I also have some sense that this is true for others. For T-group trainers, one major benefit gained from conducting a laboratory is having intensive contact with other trainers. As another example, I served for some time as a consultant to an internal consultant in a company, and one of my major functions was simply to be an available professional who spoke his language. I provided someone to whom he could let off steam and talk about things in a relatively unguarded way that would be understood. In essence, I am saying here that it really is very difficult for a consultant to try to go the whole route alone; he could probably go just so far without some chance to con-

4. For instance, Sherlock Holmes has Watson, Sir Henry Merrivale has Inspector Masters, and Roderick Alleyn has Inspector Fox.

nect with others who are concerned with similar issues in the field of organizational change.

The mirror image of this process is also important: the conflict and competition which can develop between detectives (and consultants) who interact for mainly collaborative purposes. When collaboration occurs under the stress of a crisis situation, whether it be a crime or an interpersonal crisis within the organization, the outside professionals involved are also likely to experience a rise in their own emotionality, and hence the likelihood that they may create difficulties for each other. Here is an example of Commander Gideon with a colleague:

> The manner in which the words were uttered annoyed Gideon, and for the first time, he thought: *I'm going to have to watch him.* He stared into Cox's very bright dark-blue eyes, and read the defiance in them. If he used the wrong tactics now he might make co-operation extremely difficult, and he had plenty to do without adding a kind of departmental feud. [Marric 1963, p. 26]

Consultants are likely to create similar problems for one another, particularly when feelings run high, and it is difficult to know whether or not you are being truly effective with the client. A consulting colleague offers an easier, safer target for pent-up feelings. This release can be useful *if* there is enough open processing to keep it manageable, as noted in chapter seven.

Sequential and Parallel Cases

One final dimension of the detective and consulting roles was suggested to me by the *differences* among detectives rather than by a basic pattern common to all of the them. This is the question of whether the detective works on cases one at a time; in sequence; or on several cases at once, in parallel. Most of the detectives whom I have read about tend to work on the sequential model, but J. J. Marric's George Gideon is a notable exception to this rule. In fact, one of the main attractions of his books to me is the number of different cases in which he is involved at once, and the ways in which his thinking about one case produces ideas or new directions for another which is continuing at the same time.

I think this same variation exists in terms of the consultant's process. Working on several cases in parallel can lead to many conflicts in terms of time and energy and in terms of emotional commitment to several systems. On the other hand, I seem to be drawn toward these kinds of conflicts, and I apparently like having to make those kinds of choices. I find that working on several cases in parallel leads to getting more ideas about each than I would if I were working in one client system at a time. My experiences in one setting seem to trigger off new ideas or new ways of looking at the experiences that I am having in another, and I feel that they build upon each other in a way that they couldn't if they were taken over more extended periods or separated times.

It is not clear to me that there is really a "best" position for a consultant on this particular dimension. I can also see advantages to working in sequence, because it does cut down on the demands in terms of output of conflicting time and inputs of energy, and also because it provides one with a chance to stop and think a bit about the previous case before moving on to another. This may lead to better planning than would have occurred if both were happening at the same time. The choice of sequential versus parallel cases should probably depend on several factors, such as the personality and stage of development of the consultant, the needs of a particular phase in a client system, and other demands which life makes on the consultant.

Conclusions

At this point, I should like to summarize very briefly what has been written and sketch out one or two patterns which seem to emerge. I have looked at the attributes of the role of the fictional British detectives and tried articulate points where it seemed to me to be analogous to that of the behavioral science oriented organizational change consultant. One major theme was that both roles seemed to have several attributes which I find to be emotionally satisfying and which I am guessing may also be a positive force on other consultants: the temporary nature of involvement in a system, the concentration on gathering evidence and trying to solve the puzzles which it represents, the potential for "dramatics," the potential for action and the excitement it contains, the stance of "expert" in behavioral science, and the stimulation of working on several cases at once. It was suggested that each of these satisfactions, while important, carried potential dangers in terms of making it more difficult to reach the major task goal of the consulting process, which is to improve the capabilities and functioning of the client system. Several other demands of the consultant role were described, and these might be seen as ways of keeping the above satisfactions from getting out of hand: promoting consciousness of self; avoiding incorporation into the client system; arranging for some collaborator or sounding board with whom to check perceptions, ideas, and feelings; using intuition as one means of generating ways to understand the situation; and being wary of the tendency to lump people into the oversimplified categories of "good" and "bad."

There are also two general questions relating to consulting which seemed to come up again and again as I thought about the above categories. The first one is well known: How does a consultant facilitate the obtaining of *informational inputs* to his "detection" process? How does he get valid information from the organization and its members, ideas they may have about problem solutions, useful ideas from behavioral science in general, outside views of his own operation, and new ways of his own for looking at the situation? Several means have been suggested, such as an intuitive stance, parallel cases, action intervention, a focus on evidence, self-consciousness, and collaboration (both with clients and with external professionals). One implication of this chapter is that there are some tensions among these various means of getting inputs. For instance, an active step (such as immediate feedback to a working group) which is too threatening may lead to the clients defining themselves as "suspects" and consequently cause them to eliminate or distort the information they communicate to the consultant. This suggests the obvious point that the degree of *trust* between the client and the consultant will be an important determinant of the consultant's success at being able to accurately perceive reality in a given consulting situation.[5]

Less obvious, perhaps, is the notion that the consultant's trust of *himself* is also a factor in this search for useful definitions of the situation. He needs this trust in order to be willing to look at the data which his own self-consciousness will generate. He also needs it in order that his own anxiety about getting a viable view of the situation not block him from obtaining new views through following events wherever they lead, that is, to look at the client system for some period with an intuitive stance requires some confidence on the consultant's part that something *will* come out of this free period, that a total blank will not be drawn. This may seem like an unnecessary elaboration of a simple point, but I think that this lack of trust in self may be at least part of the reason why some consultants tend to go into an organization with a relatively solidified view of what they will find; a view which sometimes proves not to be very useful but can be held to very tenaciously.

This brings me to the second general question which is relevant here: How does the consultant *balance his professional needs with his other personal needs?* For example, how does he get satisfaction in terms of feeling competent, being active, being central, being held in high esteem by the clients, et cetera, without blocking or overshadowing the clients' view of themselves and thereby limiting possibilities for growth in the client system? I have suggested that the

5. I had originally assumed that the question of trust was a point (like many others not discussed in this chapter due to limitation of space) where the analogy between the detective and the consultant was not relevant. It became clear, however, that although the detective often starts out operating on a model of *mistrust*, the costs to him are the same as to the consultant: it becomes much more difficult to get accurate data from participants in the situation or help in solving the mystery.

consultant can strive for self-awareness and getting data from others as ways of testing why he is doing something at a given moment. This does not mean that he should discard some behavior just because it is personally gratifying to him; that would be removing many of the very reasons why the consultant has chosen to play this particular role. Rather, it suggests trying to choose based on a view of integrating both the professional and the personal, a process that I think is quite possible given the high motivation toward professional competence of many of the consultants with whom I am acquainted.

Finally, there is an interesting similarity in role structure between detective and consultant which the writing of this chapter has clarified for me. Expressed simply, the detective (consultant) is able to develop a certain amount of credibility and connectedness with those involved in a mystery (the particular members of an organizational unit) because of his structural position. At least for the amateur detectives, they represent some general societal values, such as truth and justice (effectiveness, organizational and individual health) without being an official member of the governmental hierarchy, for example, the police department (or the top management of the organization.) Both the detective and the consultant then, tend to be seen as not having a particular vested interest to uphold other than getting at the truth of a situation. When this disinterest is doubted, each has a much more difficult task, usually because of interference from those most concerned.[6]

In terms of the process of this chapter, I would also like to repeat my beginning suggestion: as a part of the continuing search for better understanding of the organizational change consultant and his process, one useful strategy seems to me

6. The vested interests of the police are partly created by the government agency most concerned about public opinion, while the stockholders' opinion is the threat in many organizations. Both these groups of people are usually very far removed from the actual facts of a case and therefore call for mainly image projection rather than effectiveness.

to look at the interests and peripheral characteristics of those who are drawn to consulting. Not, as in the case of much of the early leadership literature, only to see what makes a "good" consultant, but rather to discover and articulate new dimensions of the consultant's role.

9. The Scene of the Crime:
The Ecology of Consultation

The previous chapter examined some hidden consequences of the consultant's role, especially those which result from the consultant's satisfaction of his own needs at the expense of criminating the client or making him overly dependent on him. This continues a double threaded theme which runs throughout the book: *how* consultants operate (technique and consequences) and *why* they should operate one way versus any other (values and professional identity). Other writers, such as Schein (1969), Harrison (1970), and Argyris (1970) have also discussed these issues together.

In spite of this attention to the hows and whys of consulting, there is one aspect which has been almost totally ignored: the *wheres* of consulting. There has been almost nothing written about the impact of the immediate physical setting on the consulting process. Reports of change projects may present various kinds of data about diagnoses, interventions, and follow-up measures of subsequent behavior in the client system; but they usually include little or no information about where events took place, how settings were chosen for different consulting activities, or what the effect of the setting was on a particular process.

It has become common knowledge in the behavioral sciences that behavior is influenced by both the social setting and the physical setting in which it takes place. Behaviorally oriented consultants today are clearly aware of the social setting as an important variable in their work. I have found that very few, however, are aware of the physical setting's impact on their processes. Like American society in general, consultants in this country tend to be blind to the impact

that settings are having upon them and the client system.[1]
On a rough exploratory questionnaire I designed to get
data from consultants about how they chose the places
where different consultation events would occur, the majority of the responses were prefaced by comments such as, "I
had never thought about this before," and "This was difficult
to fill out—I don't really know how I choose my places."

The observations and ideas in this chapter are an attempt
to reduce or eliminate this blindness to physical environmental factors. From my own consulting experiences I am
convinced that the physical setting is an important piece of
the interlocking system of factors which influences the process between consultant and client. My hope is that the
following discussion will increase the reader's awareness of
the settings in which he operates and the choices he has with
respect to the selection and alteration of those settings to fit
his aims. I will begin with a very brief background discussion of the ways in which settings influence behavior and
attitudes. Then a number of issues in consulting ecology will
be explored: how decisions regarding place are made, where
data are collected, how a consultant uses his setting to present himself to the client (and vice versa), where a consultant
establishes his home base, choosing settings for different consulting activities, and influencing the setting which the consultant is using.

The Influence of Settings

Although the environment influences us in many ways, I will
present only a brief sketch here of those influences relevant
to this paper. I hope that this will be sufficient background
for the later discussions.[2]

1. See, for example, Hall's book, *The Hidden Dimension* (Garden
City, Long Island: Doubleday, 1966), which nicely documents the
effects of spatial arrangements and our blindness to them.
2. For those who wish to go deeper into environment and behavior,
I recommend H. Proshansky, W. Ittelson, and L. Rivlin, *Environmental Psychology* (New York: Holt, Rinehart & Winston, 1970);
E.T. Hall, *The Hidden Dimension* (Garden City: Doubleday, 1966);
R. Sommer, *Personal Space* (Englewood Cliffs, N.J.: Prentice-Hall,
1969); and Steele (1973).

First, I must define what I mean by *setting*. The setting referred to in this paper is the immediate physical environment surrounding the actors of interest, such as a consultant and client or a small task group meeting on a problem. Their setting includes everything which produces perceptible stimuli: the architectural features, such as walls, lights, colors; the furnishings; the physiological features such as temperature and moisture; noises and visible movements; natural features such as rocks, trees, and the like; and other human beings besides the actors, such as the other people in a park where consultant and client are talking. In all of these examples, setting refers to the physical setting, to properties which can be perceived by the actors (although they need not be consciously perceived).

Next, the issue of how settings influence people and social processes. This influence takes place in a great many ways, but we can put them into three rough categories: those influences caused by the *physical properties* of the setting, those influences caused by the *informational properties* of the setting, and those due to *emotional cues* in the setting. The physical properties of a setting help determine what people can do there: a room which is very noisy makes it difficult for more than two people to hold a conversation there, since those in a group larger than two are too far apart to be heard by one another. A table which is very small limits the kinds of tasks which can be carried out on it. If a bulletin board is placed in a hallway which is narrow and used heavily, the board will go unnoticed, since people cannot easily stop to read it without blocking traffic.

Informational properties refer to the symbolic meaning which physical objects or their qualities have for the people who use them. A Rolls Royce influences others more by its message about wealth and status than by its functioning as a physical facility. A closed door to an office has a meaning for those who wish to speak to its occupant: as a physical facility it has a handle and can be opened, but as information it often suggests that the occupant is not interested in receiving visitors. Emotional properties of settings work through the feelings, memories, and fantasies which a particular place or thing will trigger in a person. These reactions generally influence the users through the *moods* which are created by them.

Finally, both physical and informational properties have the capacity to determine attitudes and expectations of people of what will or should happen in a place. For instance, when a group of eight people enter a tavern and find that the largest table will accommodate four people, they become aware of the fact that they will probably have to split up because of a physical limitation. The same expectation can be generated when they walk in and see a sign saying, The Secret Police Considers Groups of More than Four People to be Subversive and Therefore Liable to Arrest. This piece of environmental information is even more persuasive if a policeman is standing underneath the sign. I should also note that, in my view, every physical property has some informational and emotional value in it as well. For instance, when the group enters the bar and sees only small tables, they get information about how the management expects customers to arrange themselves, and their state of mind or mood is affected by this message.

In sum, settings influence persons by facilitating or constraining what can be done in them physically; by communicating information which sets expectations and attitudes about what should normally be done in those settings; and by triggering feelings, memories, and other reactions which influence a person's mood while he is in the setting. I should also note that this process of influence is not strictly one-way. People influence the setting as well as become influenced by it. Although the emphasis in this paper is on settings as an influence or consulting processes, I will touch also on the potential available to the consultant affecting his settings as well.

Process Issues in Consultation

With this brief introduction, I will now move specifically to some of the issues which arise when considering consultation from an ecological point of view.[3] I used two main sources when developing the material for these discussions. One was interviews with colleagues about their experiences. As I said earlier, many consultants have thought very little about settings during their contacts with clients, but this did not negate the fact that they were able to recall some very interesting cases of the impact of the setting on what they were trying to do.

The second source was my own experience in consulting work. For about eight months I kept a log sheet of each experience, the nature of the setting, the apparent connections between the setting and what happened, and the process by which that particular setting was chosen. I also wrote up, from memory, sheets for previous experiences using the same headings. I must say that it was embarassing to look at how few times I had had a conscious influence over the setting for a contact or special event of some kind with a client system.

How Decisions about Place Are Made

First, a very short look at some of the factors which determine where consultants do their work. These are by no means all the possible reasons why a particular place would be chosen, but they are the major ones which have emerged from my questionnaire and interviews.

Appropriateness to the event. To begin with, it is true that some percentage of decisions about place are made based primarily on the planned event and its desired goals, as when it is decided to hold an experimental session of the board of directors *away* from the board room so that they can have more flexibility in the roles they take; or when the client's office is chosen for an initial contact in order to see him in his most frequent setting. From the standpoint of planned activities, this is the factor which should weigh most heavily

3. There are many more elaborate ways of looking at the influence of settings on behavior and attitudes. In a recent book for the Addison-Wesley Series in Organization Development (Steele 1973), I describe in detail the functions which settings perform for those who use them.

in the consultant's choices. The point of this whole chapter, however, is that in many instances appropriateness to the event may have a relatively small influence on the decision.

Tradition. In a young field, traditions are somewhat hard to come by, but I think that there are traditions in consulting, and one of them is the *off-site session* held away from the organization at a conference center or hotel. I will discuss in a later section a comparison of on- and off-site sessions. My point here is that this is an example of a pattern of choice of setting which has developed and is often used without questioning whether it really fits the needs of the particular client system in the specific instance. Groups of internal consultants within a given system or external consultants working for a management consulting firm would seem to me to be particularly susceptible to developing traditional answers to where events should be held, since they see one another in practice more than most independent consultants do and therefore transmit normative expectations more easily to one another.

Stress-Reduction. Sometimes our choice of location depends upon the stresses we are experiencing and the protection that a certain place can offer from them. A public health nurse described to me her experience in this way:

> I always go to peoples' homes to play my role as nurse. Whenever I feel low or discouraged or doubtful of whether I am making much difference, I can feel myself longing to be back at my office at the hospital. There I feel in control and I can relax; in the homes I am always in the way and not able to relax.

I think that the same process applies to consultants. The more stress or anxiety a consultant is experiencing, the more likely he is to want to be functioning on familiar ground where he can be in charge, or relax, or both. Unfortunately, stressful times often come when there are difficulties between the consultant and the client system, and this can push the consultant toward withdrawing into his own territory at precisely the times when he would make the most impact by moving outward to engage the client.

This problem is often caused because the consultant has

not established a place of his own in the client system's spaces. Various colleagues have reported feelings very similar to my own in this regard: if I do not have some place to occasionally sit down, relax, take notes, think, or whatever, the process of working in a field setting can be very fatiguing and stressful. A teacher who moves from room to room for different classes told me that she feels the same way.

As a remedy for these stresses caused by "rootlessness," I think it is important for a consultant to establish in the client system a *temporary location* which he can use without being in anyone's way. This allows time for the periodic process of rejuvenation which I believe we all need in order to function well. I should also note, however, that the choice of *where* you locate is an important one. You may be sending a symbolic message through your choice of location. I have seen a consultant locate himself in a subgroup's area and thereby cut himself off from other groups which were engaged in a dispute with his "home" group. It should be a matter of early diagnosis to determine what the major splits are in the system and how important it is to not be construed as being in someone's camp.

Personal preferences. Another factor which influences a consultant's choice of place is his own preference. I have noticed in myself a tendency to develop elaborate rationales for why a particular session or conference should be held at a resort of which I just happen to be particularly fond. I have favorite places, as do many other consultants, and I think it is legitimate to seek them out. In seeking, however, we must also be aware of what we are giving up. If a particular resort is pleasant for me but likely to create a nonwork mood in the group, then I think it doubtful that the decision should be carried by my personal preference, particularly if the client is paying for the event (as he usually is). If someone wants to come along while I take a vacation, that is another matter.

Decisions by default. From both my interviews and observations I would say that a fairly high percentage of spatial decisions are in fact made more by default than anything else. By this I mean that the client suggests I come to his office, or someone tells me that a room is available down the hall, or whatever, and I accept this with no conscious questioning of the consequences of this choice. In some instances expediency may be the most efficient way of choosing a place to meet, but the whole point of this paper is that this is an empirical question which varies from instance to instance, not an assumption to be made across the board. I think consultants need to be more aware of the choices which are being made about settings and *how* they are being made, so that it can be a problem-solving process rather than a grasping for whatever pops up first.

A second aspect of the decision-by-default pattern is that this often occurs when the client is controlling when and how we meet and I have been unwilling to openly challenge this process by questioning a location which he suggests. I believe that in order to be truly useful to the client, I must be willing to raise literally any issue concerning the process between us. The spatial decision process is no exception, and it has often been a trigger for talking about other process issues.

Settings and Data Collection

The second main issue I wish to consider is the influence of place on the process of collection of data. The general point is simple but often forgotten: where you choose to collect data will have an impact on the quality of the information you obtain. Consider the following old chestnut.

A man is crawling around at night on the grass under a street light. A policeman arrives on the scene and asks what the gentleman might be doing.

"Looking for my watch," the man replies.

"I'll help you," says the policeman, "where exactly do you think you dropped it?"

"Down by that tree," the man says as he points down the road.

"Then why are you looking for it up here?" the policeman asks.

"Because the light's so much better."

Although I like the joke, the process is exactly what I hope to avoid in consultation: I want to look for data where they are, not where it is comfortable to look for them. For instance, when I take a group to a hotel for a team-building session, it is usually a fairly effective and manageable process with an informal climate and easy discussion. The problem is that many kinds of data, such as how and when people interact as they work, cannot be seen there; that is not where they get dropped. Those data can be observed only in the relatively more cumbersome process of being around in the client system and making ad hoc interviews and observations. This is not to say that what people say in the hotel is irrelevant, only that it is incomplete unless compared with on-site observations.

Let us consider another example. If I were doing a group interview on organizational climate, I should get somewhat different responses depending on where it was held. If we meet out on the factory floor, incidents connected with the physical work will tend to be the theme; if we hold the meeting in the board of directors room, the themes would probably be either responsibility to the organization or the injustice of the social distance between workers and directors; and so on. As I will discuss more fully below, the setting influences peoples' associations and memories, and therefore also influences the train of conversations.

The kind of data a consultant is seeking should be the guide to where he seeks his evidence. The temptation to cite the analogy to a detective again is too much for me to pass up, and I see the process as similar to the detective arriving at the country house where a crime has been committed. As we would not expect him to look in another house for clues about the events that had just occurred, I do not think that a consultant should avoid looking for clues about a group's process in its own spaces, at the "scene of the crime."

As consultants, we are also trying to collect data about the individuals who make up our client systems. It is very easy to unconsciously fall into a pattern where we see individuals only in certain situations, and where we do not see them in others. Arthur Colman has provided a beautiful example of the control a pattern can exert over the view which a psychiatrist gets of a patient by seeing him only in a hospital setting.

> [In the hospital] Mr. Pond characteristically remained silent even when spoken to, except for unprovoked outbursts against the staff. . . . Quotes from the staff refer to Mr. Pond as "disturbed," "irrational," schizophrenic." . . . My contacts with Mr. Pond were marked by the sparseness of verbal communication, although there was much angry suspicious glaring on his part. He did not want to talk about himself, his wife, or the baby.

> [In contrast, Colman visited the Ponds after their baby was born] Mr. Pond greeted mc in a warm, gracious manner and asked me to call him by his first name. . . . I was offered coffee and sat down in the (one) chair; but Mr. Pond pressed me to sit with his wife on the mattress. He then took the stuffed chair and stretched out his legs so that I could not straighten mine from their cramped position without touching his. The next hour was spent in conversation controlled by Mr. Pond. The Ponds were at ease and calm in contrast to my own anxiousness in the unfamiliar and provocative surroundings. . . . At no time during the visit was Mr. Pond's relaxed and confident tone lost. Nor did I see any signs of the disturbed behaviour that had characterized his outside-home contacts. His needs for situational control, which made his behaviour so unpleasant and even bizarre in the hospital, were satisfied by the aggressive seating arrangement and the security he felt in his self-styled rooms. [1968, pp. 465–66]

In this example, Colman shows how a doctor has a tendency to generalize about people by seeing them only on the doctor's home turf, which is the hospital or doctor's office. For many consultants, the pattern is the reverse: they see a client only in the client's home territory where the client can manage all the props. The implication is quite simple: if a consultant wants to have data about the way a client handles different kinds of situations (and thereby have data about his range of needs and skills), he must be aware of when he is falling into a comfortable pattern of seeing the client in only one setting. The point is that there is no "best" place for contact with the client, and that a variety of settings are most likely to provide a well-rounded picture of the individuals and groups in the system.

Presentation of Self

The data about the client discussed above represent only one-half of the information transmitted between client and consultant. Through their contacts, the client is also learning about the consultant. For this reason, I prefer to think of their contact as a mutual process of "presentation of self" in Goffman's terms (1959), whereby they provide various cues to one another about how they wish to be seen and dealt with.

Looked at in this manner, the relevant question here is how the consultant and client use the setting to communicate images to one another. The first and most immediate way is through the setting which each carries around with him, namely, his clothes, style of grooming, and general personal appearance. Visual appearance often conditions the client's reactions to an expectation of the consultant, and vice versa. I have noticed in myself a tendency to make fairly careful choices about clothes during my first contacts with a client, so that I will not generate an unclosable psychological gap between us in his mind. As our contact continues, I am less and less careful about this, mainly because physical appearance shrinks to a smaller and smaller percentage of the total information which the client has about me. In the beginning it was close to 100 percent, and toward the end of a project it is probably less than 5 percent.

This change in the relative importance of appearance also allows me to use my own natural variations from the client's style as useful points of difference to be examined. In the beginning of a relationship, as I said, the connection is tenuous enough so that clear differences could threaten the relationship itself.

On a larger scale than clothes, the client and consultant also learn about one another from their individual home territories and personal "props," or the items which they regularly use in their territories. If they meet in the client's office, the physical setting and the way the client uses it communicates to the consultant what the client is like, at least on his home ground. The things he has put in the office tell the consultant what the client's personal preferences of style are like, as well as something about his interests.[4]

The same kinds of information are provided about the consultant if they are meeting on his home ground. Just as with clothes, there is also the problem here of communicating to the client the consultant's style without creating too large an initial gap if they are very different kinds of people. Several social workers have reported this to me as one of their recurring problems. If they decorate their offices and bring in artifacts which they feel represent their personalities, it can emphasize to a poor client that the latter is of very low economic status compared to the social worker and therefore block the development of the relationship.

Through the ways in which they *use* their settings, people also communicate particularly what they want the relationship to be. Consider this case told to me by a consultant colleague:

> It was my first contact with Mr. X [the client], and he had asked me to come to his office. It was a fairly long session, so I moved around from time to time. Every time I moved, Mr. X. moved as well. It took me a while to recognize the pattern: he was making sure that he was always just a little higher [physically] than I was. It sometimes took considerable chair shuffling and some standing up, but he managed it.

Presumably the client was concerned about relative power in his as yet uncertain contacts with the consultant, and the jockeying was his way of trying to maintain dominance or to overcome a "one-down" feeling which he already had by virtue of being a receiver of help.

This is just one example of how a person can use his

4. This is, of course, less true the more the organization has controlled these choices from above.

"props" to communicate what he wants the consulting relationship to be like. Others include the amount of distance he keeps; the formality of seating (Always behind his desk?); the use of light (If there is a glare, in whose eyes is it?); the degree to which he makes it a very private meeting through closing doors, pulling shades, et cetera; the degree of control he exerts over how others use the space; and many others.

Of course, if the meeting is taking place on the consultant's home ground then he is sending similar messages through his use of "props" and the kind of control he tries to exert over the client. Perhaps the classic example of this use of settings to establish the nature of control in the relationship is the couch in the analyst's office, whereby the analyst can see the patient, but the patient cannot see the analyst. It is significant that those therapists who now take a more flexible view of the relationship between therapist and patient also tend to throw out the couch and use their settings in more varied ways related to their therapeutic goals.

The choice of where the consultant and client choose to meet will obviously influence this process of building a relationship. In many of the examples noted above, the choice of setting played a large part in determining who was "in charge." Sometimes a neutral territory would be most useful for a beginning, followed by the client's or consultant's home territory. The choice should depend on factors such as the personal security of the consultant and client, the degree of choice which actually exists (some clients will not meet anywhere but in their office for a first session), and what kind of relationship you are trying to establish.[5]

Factors in the Setting's Impact

The mutual process of presentation of self is only one of many kinds of events which take place during a planned change project. The problems of consulting ecology relate to the degree of the appropriateness of the fit between the physical setting and a whole variety of consulting activities.

5. More will be written about this choice of where to meet in the discussion of territoriality later in this chapter.

Since this variety is so large, there is no possibility of describing the "right" setting for each activity. The determinants of fit are also too complex to establish simple rules. There are, however, several general factors which, if understood, provide good guidelines about which setting to choose in a given situation. These factors are the mood of a place, availability of data, the surrounding environment, and the impact of territoriality.

The mood of a place. One major factor in the choice of a setting is the mood which it is likely to foster in the inhabitants. As I envision a place, there are many stimuli in it: light, sounds, things, styles of decorations, and so on. These serve as cues which form symbolic messages read by the client group. These messages trigger various reactions and feelings such as memories of past events in this or similar settings, feelings about the place in terms of its pleasantness, expectations about what will or should happen in it, or personal fantasies which are internal to the person but initiated by the cues in the present setting (such as a single smell in his aunt's house sending Proust off on four volumes of reminiscences and fantasies).

I see the influence of these reactions on the consulting process as occurring mainly through the mood which they create in the members of a group. As Slater described the process, unconscious and preconscious fantasies and feelings have a tendency to affect the thematic content of a group session (1961). Here, for example, is a case from my own work:

> I was engaged in a weekend team-building workshop with a group of eight people who were in a quasiconsultant role within their organization. In one day we met in three different settings at the conference center: a lounge that was regularly used for meetings, the bedroom of one of the group members, and the library area of the center.
>
> The themes of the three sessions were interestingly different. In the lounge, which had many trappings of the parent organization, the issues discussed were responsibility, courage to take risks within the organization, and

the relationship of conscience to their role performance. In the bedroom the issues were sexuality, pairing, and intimacy relations within the group. In the library, the group talked mainly about the problem of true knowledge and the difficulties in understanding what they were trying to do and its impact.

These sessions occurred so close together and had such different themes that it seemed clear to me that the nature of the setting (as well as the group's real problems) was having an impact. It did not create the issues, but it helped determine which ones they would be thinking and feeling about and therefore would tend to discuss.

A director of training in a large organization had obviously seen similar patterns when he told me:

We have to hold our management training sessions here (at a private lodge). All our rooms at the plant have messages like "work," "look good," and "play it straight for higher management" just oozing from the walls. The whole climate there is organizational, and you can practically see the men start thinking about their place in the system as soon as they walk in. In fact, I can feel myself doing it, too!

This quote illustrates another dynamic of the mood-setting process: peoples' moods are affected by their seeing a place with which they have a past history of events. Many rooms in organizations carry this kind of meaning, such as the place where a man was chewed out by a vice-president in a "show-and-tell" meeting when he admitted that no one could be certain that a program would succeed. On returning to that room for future meetings, he would tend to experience the emotions he had felt during the earlier session.

Sometimes such feelings help the progress of the present event, and sometimes they hinder it. For instance, I wrote an article (Steele 1968c) in which I looked at two laboratory sessions held by the same organization in very different conference settings, one a campus lakeside setting and the other a ten-story town building. I attributed the difference in feelings of shared community concern (high in the former, low in the latter) partly to the physical structures of the two laboratories. After that paper appeared, a member of the second laboratory pointed out to me that I had missed one of the most significant factors which retarded community development in the second lab: there had been a lot of controversy in the system when that high-rise building had been constructed. Many members felt that the money should have gone into struggling grass-roots programs within the organization. Thus, when participants attended the second laboratory in that building, it was a visible reminder of that controversy and a trigger for feelings of hostility, resentment, and alienation from the decision-making processes of the system. This was as much a force of the setting as were other attributes I discussed in the article (low visibility, separation of meeting and eating locations, single rooms), but it worked as an influence on mood through the memories of the people using the setting. This case also suggests that a consultant usually needs to collaborate with someone inside the system in order to assess the mood which a place may effect in a client group; the consultant will not be likely to know the particular associations which a place may have for one or more members of the group.

Availability of materials and data. Earlier I discussed the consultant's need to work in settings which contain the data he is trying to collect. The same holds true for self-examination or problem-solving sessions conducted by a client group: the setting should be one (or a number, since it could change) which offers the materials necessary for what they are trying to do. Perhaps this may seem to be a very obvious statement, but this point is often forgotten when locations are chosen for planned events. Here is a simple example from my notes:

> A manager recently called me and asked if I would meet with him and his group to talk about how their physical space could be improved. He suggested that we meet in a good conference room at a nearby hotel—a setting that they had used often when they wanted to get away from the bustle of the office and talk about their process problems.

My response was that I liked the hotel generally, but for the purposes of this meeting it would have none of the data we needed, i.e., the layout and impact of their present work spaces. Instead, we held the meeting in their own offices, where we could literally point to different aspects that bothered people, could arrange chairs and try out new pathways as we thought of them, and could test noise levels and psychological impact of different places in the office by immediately going to them and talking about how they felt.

The point is that their own offices had almost all the materials and data for the problem they were tackling, while the hotel had practically none. I should note that we dealt with the bustle problem by having the switchboard take messages from phone calls, rather than put the calls through, so that the group could concentrate on the problem at hand.

All settings contain various materials, features to work with, and information by virtue of the kind of places they are. The issue in choosing a setting for a consulting activity is to specify what kinds of processes will be likely to occur and then consider which settings will be likely to help processes and which will hinder or be irrelevant to them.

I would say that consultation activities with a client group fall into three broad areas: identification and analysis of the problem, solution to the problem, and generation of commitment and motivation to deal with pressing problems or issues. These do not necessarily happen in discrete events—they usually do not—but the point is that settings can influence these processes somewhat differently. Identification of the problem often calls for a setting which has the relevant historical cues, such as with the group in the case cited from my notes, above. Generating solutions can often benefit from new and different settings which are different from the day-to-day routine and thereby help to break old patterns of assumptions about what must be done.

An example recently occurred to me which illustrates the issue so far as all three kinds of activities are concerned. This is the Aspen International Design Conference, an annual event held at Aspen, Colorado, in a very scenic part of the Rocky Mountains. One stream of discontent in recent years has been the conference's irrelevance to the really hard-nosed problems of urban design and redesign. Feelings have run quite high about this at times. Unfortunately, this may be an instance where an institution's identity is so tied up with a particular place that it will never be able to work on those kinds of problems. So long as the conference is held in Aspen, there will be no examples of these pressing urban problems to observe, nor will the conference be able to effect any live active experiments on the spot without a great deal more prior effort than would be required in a dense neighborhood in a run-down city.

So far as commitment goes, the setting tends to make it very difficult to get too worried about those problems "back there." Ironically, the setting actually provides one impetus for developing motivation: it is *so* far from the problem that those who live in the city and cannot forget the issues eventually get fed up and confront the whole conference with their anger. This suggests that a totally irrelevant setting can provide a function; but initial motivation or guilt will carry the issue just so far, and after that I believe that a more relevant setting would help.

In sum, identification of the problem, solution to the problem, and the enhancement of commitment often require somewhat different settings. It is very useful to have some idea of the goals of a session when you are planning where to have it, so that it can be made to fit the task. This also suggests that more mobility be built into consulting sessions; that more than one setting be used as the focus of the session changes. A team-building exercise might start off in the team's regular offices for a day, then shift to an isolated room to explore process and talk about new alternatives, then finish with some activities in spaces belonging to the most important interfacial groups of the team. The setting would change as the focus of activity, and therefore the materials and symbolic information required, shifts over time.

Surrounding environment. Another important factor with impact on consulting sessions is the nature of the immediate surrounding social environment, particularly whether it supports or is hostile to the activities in which you are engaged. Those consultants who arrange sites for laboratory training sessions are probably the most aware of this issue. A laboratory attempting to examine traditional societal norms in the light of new alternatives has real difficulty in creating the right experimental mood if the setting (including the people who interact with the laboratory) consistently sends messages reinforcing adherence to the norms. For example, a personal growth type of laboratory has a tough road if held in a religious center or a commercial hotel, since each has its expectations of predictable, controlled behavior. These expectations are clearly at odds with the experimental nature of the laboratory.

Predictability and impulse control is just one dimension where a bad fit can occur between a session and its surrounding environment. The *degree of formality* of dress, meeting times, and physical arrangements is another. This can be crucial in hotel settings where a consultant is trying to establish a looser mood than at work, and the hotel staff is trying to maintain a "high-class" image and therefore enforcing the very formalities which the session is trying to escape. Another dimension is the *pace* of activities. The more a setting has time demands (fixed meeting rooms available only at certain times, fixed meal times, scheduled recreational activities), the more likely there will be incongruence between that place's pace and the pace that would evolve naturally as the laboratory or session developed. Still another dimension which I have recently experienced in conflicts with facilities management is the *flexibility of living arrangements*. In some instances changeability of living patterns can be an important input to a laboratory or work session, but this is usually hampered by the surrounding culture's expectations (hotel management, et cetera) that those patterns remain fixed.

A very important aspect of fit between consulting activity and surrounding culture is the degree of *interference* between the two. For labs this takes such simple forms as a large number of other guests (nonlaboratory) at the site making it difficult to get food served in reasonable time. Another is simply interruptions which impede the sessions themselves. As I implied earlier, team-building activities are often held away from the office to reduce the interference of telephone calls and other business-as-usual contacts which break the stream of the session. I will discuss further this strategy for handling interference in the section on choosing between on- and off-site sessions.

In general, then, the point is to be aware of the fact that a laboratory or other consulting session takes place within a larger culture which may or may not be supportive of what you are trying to do. The charge is to pick those settings which are more supportive, unless the very resistance is a part of the data which you want to generate and process.

The impact of territoriality. The last factor I will mention here is the influence of territoriality on consulting sessions. I am using territoriality in the ethologists' sense of a process whereby a particular location is identified with an "owner" (or "owners"), and vice versa. Through both the encouragement of symbolic cues and familiarity with the setting, the "owner" tends to be more able to be in control of events in his own territory than he is outside it. Both he and others see it is legitimate that he be in charge when on his own home territory.

Territoriality influences the consultative process in many ways. I suggested earlier that when a consultant chooses a temporary location for his own place while doing field work, he should be aware of whose turf he is choosing, since this can affect how he is identified by the system's members.

Another process already touched upon is that of the first contact between consultant and client, and the ways this event can be influenced by where it happens. The following observation I made is a striking example of the influence of territoriality on that first contact:

A consulting team was meeting for the first time with a client group with whom they would very likely be working. The meeting was held in the formal living room of the head of the client group. As the consultants reported it later, the conversation was generally dinner-party type in subgroupings determined by the seating arrangements. The distances and positions of people were such that at no time was there an integrated conversation on one topic which included the whole group. Afterwards, the consultants complained that none of the relationship issues they had hoped to clarify were dealt with, since the meeting never really started. They also said they had feelings of frustration but also felt inhibited by the fact that they were guests in someone's living room. They knew that the event was being structured partly by the physical layout, yet they felt reluctant to "tinker" with another person's living room.

It seems safe to say that if the chairs had been arranged in a circle, the people there would have been more aware of their potential as a total group. But the important feature of this was the fact that the layout was *left* that way and allowed to control the conversation. Once the consultants agreed to that setting for the meeting, they were fated to be in someone else's territory and therefore to feel constrained as to how much control they could freely exert over the setting itself. In this case, they felt the risks were too high to attempt to influence the arrangement. This was probably unfortunate, because to at least raise the issue of goals of the session and make the setting fit them would have allowed the possibility of mutual influence as well as modeled the consultants' own value of open problem solving as applied to process issues.

Since control is a central fact of life for every organization, territoriality is obviously a live phenomenon for client systems from day to day, not just when the consultant is at work. Often consultation decisions about location interact with the history of the way locations have been chosen before. Another example from my own consultation notes:

When I was working with a client group made up of two subgroups, A and B, which were twenty miles apart in location, the issue arose of where we would hold a joint session looking at intergroup problems. There was some pressure on me to hold it at A. Then it emerged that when these two groups got together, they always did it at A, ostensibly because that was where the mutual boss of the two groups was located and it was therefore "more efficient." The members from B felt that they were always making the accommodation to travel and therefore playing second fiddle to A.

Since this problem was one aspect of what we were examining, we decided to experiment and hold the session at B. The B members were more active and leveling than usual (no doubt due to the type of session as well as the setting); more importantly, the system found that holding it as B was not inefficient—only the mythology of the system and A's vested interests in feeling one-up had supported that view. They now mix up the pattern of meeting locations, as well as discussing issues of power and control more openly. They do not need the territorial message as a safe and indirect means of communication.

There are endless examples of similar patterns in organizations, where territoriality gets used as a vehicle for maintaining control or sending messages about relative status. The point here is that the consultant should be aware of this process as a force for change, as a clue to underlying feelings about status, and as an issue in choosing where his own consulting activities should occur.[6]

The On-Site–Off-Site Choice

In the previous section I have considered some of the major factors which should be considered when choosing a setting for different kinds of consulting contact between consultant and client. There is one issue which has arisen either directly or by implication throughout this whole discussion, and its frequency makes it worth some direct attention. This is the decision of whether to hold a session such as a problem-solving meeting, team-building event, or whatever on-site (in the client system's own spaces) or off-site (at some conference center, hotel, or other place not connected

6. For a more complete review of the concept of territoriality, see Altman's article (1970).

directly with the organization). For convenience, I will refer to these alternatives as ON and OFF, respectively.

In the growth of organization development as a field, the notion of the OFF session has developed into somewhat of an institution. I believe it has become almost a given for many consultants and many client systems that process types of sessions or OD (organization development) activities in general should be held OFF rather than ON. I think that this assumption is mistaken, and that like any other choice in the consulting process there is a mixture of effects of doing a session in one place rather than another.

Recently I have been doing more interventions and laboratorylike sessions ON, because I think they have advantages and because I want to gain some experience with that process. These are some of the effects which have emerged, described in the form of the advantages of OFF and ON.

Advantages of OFF. One motive for going OFF for a session is that it tends to create a mood of exploration, contemplation, and "stepping outside" (literally) to look at what has been happening from day to day. This reflective mood can be set quite nicely by going to a retreat away from the scene of the wars of work.

A second but related advantage to OFF, and the one which is most often mentioned to me in interviews or questionnaires, is that it removes *interference* with the task at hand. If people are not in their regular office, they are not interrupted by telephone calls, people dropping in, and other demands of their day-to-day work roles. This allows them a greater chance to focus their attention on process and/or longer-term planning issues.

An OFF location also removes the participants from being *observed* by other members of the organization, including groups which may be hostile to the OD process. This removal from scrutiny can help the participants to be less inhibited than they would be in full view of others. It has the related disadvantage, however, of removing a group from the system: often their *absence* is very visible and generates many speculations and rumors about what they are doing.

One of the original notions of the OFF session was the

cultural island concept in laboratory training (Schein & Bennis 1965, chapter sixteen). In this view, getting away helps *unfreeze old behavior patterns,* attitudes, and assumptions, giving the person an opportunity for a fresh start. A session held OFF does not have all the surrounding cues of the regular work setting about good, acceptable, or expected behaviors. This may help the participants to think in new ways, relate in more varied ways, and generate new alternatives for problems.

The final advantage can be thought of as providing new social materials (through physical symbolic cues). An OFF location can also provide new *physical* materials for experimenting with space, color, and arrangements with more freedom than the participants would have in their regular spaces.

Advantages of ON. One advantage of sessions in regular work spaces has been mentioned early in the chapter: ON sessions have a rich array of cues about problems and processes. The data are there, not down the block. When people talk about patterns of interaction or bad arrangements they can demonstrate or look to see if the descriptions are accurate. The ON location tends to highlight awareness of the processes which exist (in contrast to the OFF effect of stimulating new possibilities).

Another advantage is that the live settings are available to be *manipulated* if someone wants to see what difference a new arrangement would make. This can change the way spaces are arranged.

Related to this is one of the most interesting advantages of ON: special events in a system's spaces can change the way those spaces are *used* and enhance the creative utilization of facilities in general. A colleague reported to me that after we did a three-day laboratory in a school's own settings, the common room where we had held general sessions during the laboratory became a regular gathering place for the school community in the morning before classes. This was doubly significant, because before the laboratory people just did not get together anywhere at that time. Similarly, community development programs can have a double payoff if they illustrate a variety of uses for the community's own spaces. Holding a community development session OFF tends to contribute nothing to this kind of better use of resources.

ON sessions also provide *more realistic pictures* of peoples' involvement in the OD process. In one ON session we did, which was aimed at an organizational diagnosis with a 250-member system in the members' own offices, we could see participation build up or drop off as people either became engaged in the program or went back to their desks. In OFF sessions people tend to make one choice, to be there or not, and then to look more or less as though they are in it even if psychologically they are not. The ON session raises the question of the continuing choice to be involved or to be back at one's regular activities: this presents both a more difficult session (in terms of smoothness) and a more reality-centered one where data on involvement are visible and therefore workable.

Finally, the most important advantage of the ON session is very likely the message it sends about *where and when* issues should be confronted and the process analyzed. The symbolic message of the choice of ON as a site for a team-building session, for instance, is that these kinds of process discussions can occur in regular work settings. Conversely, the most potent single message of the OFF team-building session may well be that if you want to deal with process problems or more direct confrontation, you should go away from the work setting and do it on nonwork time. This to me has a high cost, since one goal of consultation is to help the system develop capabilities to deal with problems when it will make the most difference. This includes freeing the system to design special events, but it also should include legitimizing dealing with issues in real time rather than saving them up for a big blow-off. OFF sessions tend to encourage saving up, and ON sessions imply that these issues can be dealt with in real time, since they are associated with the regular work place.

These, then, are some of the considerations which influence the ON or OFF choice. I should add, however, that the discussion could be misleading in the black-or-white way in which I have presented it. Rather than being strictly either/or situations, the advantages described are really examples of *dimensions* which need to be considered in designing a site for a session. For example, OFF has an advantage usually in being out of the range of interference from telephone calls, visits, et cetera; but this is not the exclusive property of OFF sessions, it is just easier with them. If one wants the greater real data of an ON session and low interference, this is a problem to be solved, not an inherent impossibility. For the ON organization exercise described above, we dealt with the *buffering from interference* problem by setting up screening devices for telephone and face-to-face contacts. For the exercise, this served the same purpose as meeting away from the office. The difference from usual ON practice was that buffering was taken as an issue, rather than as the given that the only way to get this is to use an OFF location.

Influencing the Setting

Throughout this chapter, the primary message has been that the consultant should be aware of his selection process when choosing settings for his activities. This is because the physical setting serves as an independent variable having an impact on attitudes, mood, and behavior. It would be a mistake, however, to assume that this influence process goes only one way. Attitudes and moods also serve as motivations to behavior which changes settings. In this latter case the nature of the setting is the dependent variable, influenced by the things which people do to it.

This suggests that the consultant who takes an ecological viewpoint toward his work is not merely concerned about how he *selects* settings, he also is aware of the extent to which he *influences* settings to make them appropriate for his and the client's goals. Although I have considered space to be too short to deal with this half of the influence process here, I do not mean to imply that it is less important than the selection process. I recommend to those who are interested that they read my chapters on environmental competence in Steele (1973), where I discuss the forces which block the influence of settings and lead to a "pseudofixed feature" assumption about features of the settings which are in fact changeable. Included in that discussion are some exercises which are designed to enhance a person's awareness of his style in relating to his settings.

Conclusions

My main process goal in writing this chapter has been to make consultants and clients more aware of the multiplicity of forces which affect a given planned change event, particularly focusing attention on the nature of the physical setting. Two points which I hope have been of some value are the sense that there are identifiable dimensions to be used in selecting and influencing settings, and that places should be compared on dimensions relevant to what you are trying to do. The following are among the dimensions or attributes which have emerged as likely to be relevant.

(1) *Intrusiveness:* the extent to which other people or activities will interfere

(2) *Supportiveness:* the surrounding culture's support or lack of support of what you are doing

(3) *Creature comforts:* heat, light, living spaces et cetera, and the extent to which they intrude on the activities

(4) *Mood:* the symbolic cues in the setting and what moods they are likely to foster or inhibit

(5) *Observability:* the visibility of the client group to one another and to nonparticipants

(6) *Historical cues:* people's past experiences with a place and their impact on their feelings in that place

(7) *Flexibility:* the range of ways in which a place can be used or arranged, and the variations in living arrangements which are possible

(8) *Formality:* the demands of the setting in terms of conventional behavior, routines, and the like.

(9) *Presentation of self:* the cues in a setting about those (clients or consultants) who are using it

(10) *Accessibility or remoteness:* the energy or time it takes to get to a place

(11) *Excitation or disruption:* the extent to which a setting is so different or new that it requires a good deal of time to get used to it and get down to productive work

Of course, which ones of these (or other) dimensions will be critical for a given situation is an empirical question, but one which I think is more likely to be asked and answered if you are aware of the implications of your setting for yourself and the clients.

There are several other practical implications which I would like to mention in closing. For one, I have come to the view that the physical setting is a good arena for practice in general problem solving. Its visible, concrete nature means that changes can be seen and consequences observed more easily than in many social processes. This view is supported by Piaget's findings that a young child engages in his first real learning processes through the medium of his physical environment. I believe that this process does not stop with childhood, and the environment can be used as a stimulus for learning throughout life. For instance, problem solving by a group about choosing or altering physical settings helps train the members in paying systematic attention to questions such as What are we trying to do in this session? What are our goals? What activities will we use to reach them? What kinds of settings will facilitate those activities? and so on.

Another implication of the discussion is that in the use of physical settings, the consultant's attention to his medium may at times be his most important message to the client system. If he is aware of the impact of environment and demonstrates it through creative problem solving about settings, this models in a visible way process goals which he has for the client: clearer definition of the problem, recognition of factors which influence the problem, and creativity in generating and experimenting with new alternatives. Conversely, if he does not consciously deal with the setting, as the consulting team did not when in the client's living room, he tends to dilute all the verbal exhortations which he may be directing at the client to be more aware of choices and alternatives.

This last point applies not only to individual consultants but to change-oriented institutions as well. I believe that systems such as consulting firms and community change agencies should use their facilities as laboratories in change technology; something which does not happen very frequently. The advantages of an ecological stance on the part of a change-oriented system come from two levels. One is the learning which occurs as its members experiment with their own settings. The second is the message which is sent to clients and to the surrounding community: a visible, in-process reminder of what the system is about, and the extent to which it values change and experimentation.

10. Learning and Designing:
The Business of Consulting

As I wrote at the beginning of this book, my intention was not to present an integrated theory either of change or of the consultant-client relationship. My aim was rather to consider some areas of the consultation function which had generally been overlooked in terms of systematic analysis. In considering consulting process areas such as roles, sensitivity to physical settings, and using laboratory methods for training, however, some explicit theories about effective consultant behavior do begin to emerge. In this final chapter, as a means of summarizing, I should like to briefly flesh out these theories, or at least flush them out of hiding so that they become a little more explicit.

Learning as an Organizing Principle

The most common theme throughout the book has been the importance of *learning* as the essence of the consulting process: learning by the client as being intimately connected with change and improvement, and learning by the consultant as being necessary for both current influence on the client and long-term effectiveness as situations change. This is hardly a new and surprising theme, since learning can either precede or follow change but must be connected with it somehow if lasting change is to occur. What I do think is newer here is the picture which has been developed of some of the major factors which facilitate or inhibit learning by clients and consultants.

Take for a moment the very simple chain of interaction shown in figure 13. One way of distilling the essence of what

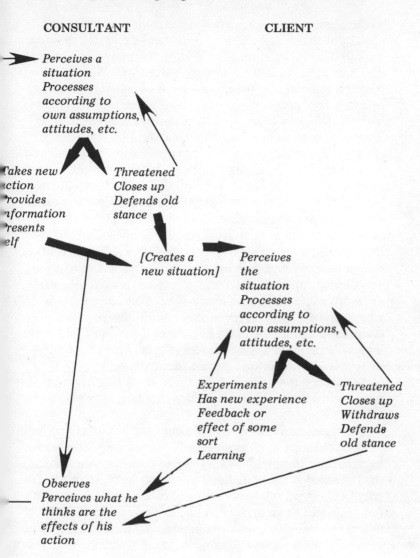

CONSULTANT   CLIENT

Perceives a
situation
Processes
according to
own assumptions,
attitudes, etc.

Takes new
action
Provides
information
Presents
self

Threatened
Closes up
Defends old
stance

[Creates a
new situation]

Perceives
the
situation
Processes
according to
own assumptions,
attitudes, etc.

Experiments
Has new experience
Feedback or
effect of some
sort
Learning

Threatened
Closes up
Withdraws
Defends
old stance

Observes
Perceives what he
thinks are the
effects of his
action

FIG. 13. One Aspect of Consultant-Client Interaction

a consultant (someone playing a consulting function at a particular time)[1] does is to assume that he changes the status quo, that as a minimum contribution he changes the *client's* (the person being helped) situation somehow. This may be through some *action* the consultant takes, through *information* or a new *point of view* he provides, or simply from his *presence* alone, which provides a sense of security and/or a signal that change is legitimate and appropriate. This changed situation is then reacted to by the client (or clients), who either uses the change as the basis for some new, experimental behavior or resists the situation by trying to change it back to the status quo, or by simply withdrawing, in either case defending the previous state of affairs. Either of these choices creates the next situation for the consultant, who then has the choice of whether or not *he* perceives the situation accurately and then either experiments or withdraws and defends himself.

In this cycle, the client learns if he takes action which gives him new information about himself, his problems, or the process of change itself. Likewise, the consultant learns if he gets feedback about the real effects of his actions and integrates that feedback into an adequate model of what forces caused the observed reactions (including his own). No learning takes place if both parties simply close themselves off and defend their original positions.

This *closed equilibrium* represents one of the traps which must be avoided in consultation. The only way I know to keep it from stabilizing is for there to be self-correction in the behavior of the consultant as he gets feedback about his effectiveness. If he chooses to deny or ignore such data, or not to collect them in the first place, then he is not likely to be able to rectify a consultation project which has begun to go off the track. This can also freeze the position of the client into one of defending old ways of doing things.

1. As I noted in the beginning this qualification is necessary, because I have tried to speak in terms of consulting behaviors and functions which can be appropriate for people in many more positions than simply the formal consultant's role.

The Process Focus

The lack of a process focus is not a surprising pitfall, since it is often the same lack of self-corrective mechanisms which leads client systems to need consultation in the first place. In my view, the major goal of a behaviorally oriented consultant should be to facilitate the development of better self-corrective processes in the client system. This type of change will have a much greater cumulative effect over the long term than will any specific structural change. I believe that the solution of specific structural or technical problems is relevant in behavioral consulting, but mainly when done in the context of a plan to improve the process whereby the system solves these kinds of problems for itself in a non-crisis manner.

In the same manner, a focus on the goal of improving system process puts a great premium on a consultant's awareness of *his own process*. This process, such as how he deals with information which disconfirms one of his theories about power in organizations, serves as an informational input to the client. The consultant provides a model, implicitly, by his own handling of his task, and that model either confirms or denies the messages he sends the client directly about how an effective human system should operate. From the discussions in this book, we should conclude that one of the most important messages he sends is about his own processes of learning (or not learning) from experience.

Learning is not important for the consultant simply as a means for modeling effective behavior to the client. It is also an essential to long-term effectiveness as a consultant. Given the embryonic state of the field, the changing conditions of different projects, the slow and sometimes unreliable feedback cycles, the ambiguous standards for what makes a consultant an effective professional, and the changes which occur in himself as a result of work which can often be emotionally stressful, any consultant who is not effective at using his experiences for learning is likely to become obsolete very quickly, even if he does not admit it for a while.

Overlapping Systems

Much of this book was written with the goal of helping those who play consultant types of roles to avoid that state of obsolescence. Specifically, I believe that an essential ingredient in learning from events and experiences is to have a relatively clear and complete picture of the essential factors which influenced the event. For a person acting as a consultant to a client system, these factors can be thought of as a set of overlapping subsystems which combine and interact to make up the universe of influences which are relevant to that experience. Although I by no means discussed them all in this book, I did try to select some of the subsystems which have tended to be less visible in previous analyses of the consulting process, including:

(1) The settings in which consultation events take place
(2) The processes through which settings are chosen
(3) The personal presentation of self between consultant and client (including clothes)
(4) The climate and dynamics of a consulting team
(5) Role expectations associated with the label *consultant,* including consultant's fantasies of self as a detective or whatever; role expectations for the label *client*
(6) Personal needs systems in consultant and their influence on his stance as a consultant
(7) The training systems whereby consultants are learning to be consultants and clients are learning to be clients
(8) The sequences of experience for both consultant and client, and whether these sequences facilitate or block learning

There are other important factors, such as modes of consultant influence, the nature of the client system power structure, the surrounding economic or political environment, and the readiness for change in a client system, which I did not discuss here. These are no less important; they just have been examined more in the past.

The theme which I have tried to stress here is that it is all too easy, given the pressures and demands of the consulting role, to lose sight of or be blind in the first place, to many of these systems of forces. This does not make them less influential, however, and blindness to them means that you are trying to generalize about events by using data from only part of the universe which produced those events; a process which is likely to produce variable results, to say the least.

For example, I once did a program for an organization which progressed very slowly until we changed our meeting room. The old one reminded participants of their "show-and-tell" room at the office and was depressing them, while I was assuming at first that it was the content of the session. If I had not hit upon the notion of the setting as an influence, I would have gone away from the program with some new learning about a meeting design which did not work, but I would have left out a major factor in why it did not: the physical setting and its symbolic information.

The Consultant as Designer

This brings me to the second major theme of the essays, the most crucial role which a consultant plays. In the introduction, I listed many different kinds of roles played when consulting: detective, ritual pig, barbarian, and so on. Yet there is one role which I believe to be superordinate, to be the main influence on these other roles. I have throughout the book made process suggestions which stem directly from this role, the role of *designer of sociopsychological experiences* for himself and clients. A consultant may be a capable diagnostician or a good teacher of behavioral science theories about healthy system behavior, but I do not think he will make very much real difference to a client system unless he is able to design sequences of events and experiences which will help both the client and himself learn new skills and new processes for doing their work.

It is the designer's role which must put together the sequences in which the consultant serves as a detective or barbarian. It is the designer's role which is involved in the collaboration with the client to establish long-range steps toward organization development. And it is the designer's role which should be operating when the consultant makes choices about the nature and sequence of tasks (and therefore experiences) which he himself undertakes.

For instance, in the chapter on consultant learning, one of the issues discussed was the tendency of consultants to cram so many live, active experiences into their schedules that they drive out the opportunity to reflect and process the experiences, thus reducing their learning. This is, in essence, a design problem; and the suggestion made there was that the consultant apply to himself the same experiential design skills that he more usually applies to the client system. In the chapter on physical settings, the theme was the need for greater awareness of design opportunities with both the client system and the consultant himself, and similarly in the chapters on consultant teamwork and on costumes.

In the same vein, the chapter on the laboratory method was intended in part to be an examination of one powerful tool for developing sociopsychological design skills. My experience with colleagues suggests that those who have a background in laboratory training are more likely to think of the facilitation of change as a process of designing experiences which the person then uses for his own learning in his own ways, while more traditional psychologists or management consultants tend to think in terms of what they can do for or give to the client, with less emphasis on how the actual process of learning will occur.

I do not mean to imply by this that an effective consultant should not supply rather concrete help to the client. On the contrary, depending on the situation he may use a wide range of media: theories about organizational and group behavior, outside views of the client's situation and problems, possible solutions to these problems, personal energy for change efforts, new structural ideas which alter process when put into effect, the gathering or redistribution of information which the system contains but does not make available to itself, curiosity about human behavior which engages others and makes them more curious, and simply his presence as a legitimation of change in the system. All of these are commodities which can be quite useful in the right mix, but it is the mixing process which is the key. That is where the consultant must use his design skills, to operate as a *social inventor,* creating new gatherings, events, or sequences of events so that the status quo no longer holds and helping these new events to occur in such a way that people experiment with them rather than withdraw and learn nothing new.

Essential to playing a useful design role is the notion that in the end the client *himself* must have an experience if he is to learn from it, no one can have it for him and then tell him what he has learned. As I indicated in chapter eight, it is all too easy for the consultant to forget for whom the events are happening and to get wrapped up in his own need for exciting experiences and dramatic postures to the detriment of the client's experiencing himself as an actor in the situation.

A focus on the designer-inventor role can help the consultant keep it before him that the client is more than an audience, that he must be an active part of the play of events. Similarly, the designer-inventor focus can help a consultant keep track of how his own needs are being served, especially his need to learn and grow as a person and a professional. This will happen only if he applies his design skills to his own life.

A Balancing Process

Finally, throughout the book there have been references to conflicting pressures of various kinds which a consultant experiences: expectations of others, self-expectation, conflicting needs of his own, demands of a particular client situation, alternative reactions to a stressful situation, and so on. Of course, it is not unique to the consulting role to be confronted with dimensions on which you must choose where you will operate; this is part of the human condition. I do believe, however, that in assuming a consultation role those choices become more obvious and more demanding. This is due to the stress of trying to induce change: the mixed feelings and reactions this causes in others, and the mixed feelings generated in the consultant by taking risks in an area where he may be on the receiving end of emotional reactions to his behavior, reactions ranging from joyful acceptance to immediate anger to stony silence and being ignored.

For the consultant who is consistently attempting to explore new ways of effecting change and developing new models of effective change agent behavior, his world can feel like a very ambiguous one, with shimmering standards which change with the light of the moment. Throughout the book I have referred to dimensions of choice which are specific to consulting. Awareness of these dimensions can help a consultant in his process of balancing conflicting pressures. Very briefly, the main choice dimensions have been:

(1) Emphasizing your own potency versus drawing out the potency of the client

(2) Choosing situations to maximize short-term performance versus choosing for long-term growth

(3) Choosing actions which emphasize performance versus actions which facilitate growth

(4) Being a corrector of "criminal behavior" versus a facilitator of experimental behavior by clients

(5) Being a provider of information (expert) versus a catalyst for information sharing between self and client or client and client

(6) Having a closed conceptual scheme versus having no preformed framework when going into a new situation

(7) Being a paid helper with a formal client versus being an advocate of needed change, even if no client exists

(8) Working alone versus working with a team

(9) Framing intense situations in a serious light versus sensing and using the humorous side of such situations

(10) Using data from the external situation versus sens-

ing and trusting internal data of feelings, intuitions, et cetera

(11) Having active experiences versus reflecting on and processing those experiences for learning

For these and similar kinds of choices, I do not see playing the consulting role as a problem of picking the "right" alternatives. The issue is rather what *balance* or mix of the alternatives will be useful and appropriate for a particular consultant. The best balance will depend on several factors. For one, the *needs of the client system* determine the problem of change itself, and this should influence the stance the consultant takes. For another, the consultant's own *personal style* will always influence the balance: how he likes to spend his time, how much acclaim he needs in order to feel secure, which aspects of himself he sees as core attributes which define him as a person, and so on. Perhaps most influential should be the particular *stage of development* of the consultant at the time, how deeply and in which areas he has developed his skills, combined with some picture, however rough, of where he sees his development heading in the long run. The term I have used for this aspect of the balancing process is *running your own race:* designing situations, experiences, and challenges (and choosing positions on the various balancing dimensions) which fit your own personal phase of development and long-term goals, rather than mirroring those of someone else. No matter how important a colleague, client, or friend may be to you, he is *not* you, and therefore his choices cannot really be used as standards for your own.

The Compleat Consultant

I doubt very much that there is any such thing as the "ideal" consultant. The necessary attributes vary too much with the kinds of situational and personal differences I have just been discussing. But in another sense, this whole book has been an exposition of my own personal view of the key process attributes which will be most effective for someone playing a consultant's role. For one, there should be an emphasis on client learning, as opposed to coercion of the client to adopt prescribed "right" attitudes and feelings. For another, there should be a strong awareness of the consultant's own learning process and continuing efforts made to make it more effective. Low consultant learning in the present is short-changing clients of the future. The consultant should apply the same skills to his own development that he uses in the service of the client's growth. As an aid to both client and consultant learning, there should be a strong awareness of the sociopsychological experience design function, whereby the consultant facilitates learning. As a part of this awareness, he should have a broad view of the forces which influence different events and situations, including such less-visible forces as the physical setting and the guilt feelings of various participants. And, finally, there should be a level of internal freedom and security which allows the consultant to see and use the ironic, humorous sides of his and others' situations as well as those aspects which are serious and demanding. I believe that learning is an essential input to consulting, and that play is an essential ingredient for learning.

References

Allingham, M. 1950. *Sweet danger*. Harmondsworth, Middlesex: Penguin.

Altman, I. 1970. Territorial behavior in humans: an analysis of the concept. In *Spatial behavior in older people,* ed. L. Pastalan and D. Carson Ann Arbor: Univ. of Michigan Press–Wayne State Univ. Press.

Argyris, C. 1961. Explorations in consulting-client relationships. *Human Organization* 20:121–33.

———. 1964. *Integrating the individual and the organization.* New York: Wiley.

———. 1970. *Intervention theory and method.* Reading, Mass.: Addison-Wesley.

Bennis, W. 1966. *Changing organizations.* New York: McGraw-Hill.

Bennis, W.; Schein, E.; Berlew, D.; and Steele, F. 1973. *Interpersonal dynamics.* 3rd ed. Homewood, Ill.: Dorsey Press.

Blake, R.; and Mouton, J. 1967. Reactions to intergroup competition under win-lose conditions. *Management Science* 7:420–35.

Bradford, L.; Gibb, J.; and Benne, K. 1964. *T-Group theory and laboratory method.* New York: Wiley.

Buhler, C. 1962. *Values in psycho-therapy.* Glencoe, Ill.: The Free Press.

Carr, J.D. 1962. *The blind barber.* New York: Collier.

Colman, A. 1968. Territoriality in man: a comparison of behavior in home and hospital. *American Journal of Orthopsychiatry* 38:464–68.

Dickson, C. 1951. *A graveyard to let,* New York: William Morrow.

Eiseley, L. 1967. Poem in *The Sierra Club Bulletin* 52.

Gladstone, A., and Burkham, D. 1966. A method of studying the relationship between pathological excitement and hidden staff disagreement. *Psychiatry* 29:106–15.

Harrison, R. 1970. Choosing the depth of organizational intervention. *Journal of Applied Behavioral Science* 6:181–202.

Harvey, J.; Oshry, B.; and Watson, G. 1970. A design for a laboratory exploring issues of organization. *Journal of Applied Behavioral Science* 6:401–12.

Harvey, O.; Hunt, D.; and Schroder, H. 1961. *Conceptual systems and personality organization*. New York: Wiley.

Malamud, D., and Machover, S. 1965. *Toward self-understanding*. Springfield, Ill.: Charles C. Thomas.

Marric, J.J. 1963. *Gideon's march*. New York: Berkeley.

Marsh, N. 1966. *Killer dolphin*. London: Ngaio Marsh.

Myers, I. 1962. *Manual for the Myers-Briggs Type Indicator*. Princeton: Educational Testing Service.

Perlo, V. Arms profiteering. *The New Republic*, 7 February 1970, pp. 17–18.

Rogers, C. 1960. *On becoming a person*. Boston: Houghton-Mifflin.

Schein, E. 1969. *Process consultation*. Reading, Mass.: Addison-Wesley.

Schein, E., and Bennis, W. 1965. *Personal and organizational change through group methods: the laboratory approach*. New York: Wiley.

Schroder, H.; Driver, M.; and Streufert, S. 1967. *Human Information processing*. New York: Holt, Rinehart & Winston.

Slater, P. 1961. Displacement in groups. In *The planning of change*, ed. W. Bennis, K. Benne, and R. Chin, pp. 725–36. New York: Holt, Rinehart and Winston.

Steele, F. 1968a. Interpersonal aspects of the architect-client relationship. *Progressive Architecture* 50:132–33.

———. 1968b. Personality and the laboratory style. *The Journal of Applied Behavioral Science* 4:25–45.

———. 1968c. The impact of the physical setting on social climate at two comparable laboratory sessions. *Human Relations Training News* 12:1–3.

———. 1970. What, me study myself? *Journal of Applied Behavioral Science* 6:360–63.

———. 1972. Organizational overlearning. *Journal of Management Studies* 9:303–13.

———. 1973. *Physical settings and organization development*. Reading, Mass.: Addison-Wesley.

Truax, C., and Carkhuff, R. 1968. *Toward effective counseling and psychotherapy*. Fayetteville, Ark.: Univ. of Arkansas Press.

White, R. 1959. Motivation reconsidered: the concept of competence. *Psychological Review* 66:297–334.